The Mistakes of Yesterday, the Hopes of Tomorrow

A volume in the series

American Popular Music

EDITED BY

Rachel Rubin and Jeffrey Melnick

The Mistakes of Yesterday, the Hopes of Tomorrow

THE STORY OF THE PRISONAIRES

John Dougan

University of Massachusetts Press
Amherst & Boston

Printed in the United States of America

ISBN 978-1-55849-969-0 (paper); 968-3 (hardcover)

Designed by Jack Harrison
Set in Adobe Minion Pro with ITC Kabel display
Printed and bound by Thomson-Shore, Inc.

Library of Congress Cataloging-in-Publication Data
Dougan, John M., 1954–
The mistakes of yesterday, the hopes of tomorrow : the story of the Prisonaires / John Dougan.
p. cm. — (American popular music)
Includes bibliographical references and index.
ISBN 978-1-55849-969-0 (pbk. : alk. paper) — ISBN 978-1-55849-968-3 (library cloth : alk. paper)
1. Prisonaires (Musical group) 2. Vocal groups—United States.
3. African American singers—United States—Biography. 4. Singers—United States—Biography.
5. African American prisoners—Tennessee—Biography. 6. Prisoners—Tennessee—Biography.
7. Music in prisons—United States. 8. Popular music—Tennessee—Nashville—History and criticism.
I. Title.
ML421.P755D68 2012
782.42164092'2—dc23
[B]

2012026788

British Library Cataloguing-in-Publication Data
A catalogue record for this book is available from the British Library.

To all prisoners making music

CONTENTS

Acknowledgments ix

Prologue: Poor Old Johnnie Ray 1

1. Nashville 8
2. The Prisonaires 19
3. The Prison, the Governor, and the Warden 31
4. Men Singing Together 48
5. Music City, USA 56
6. "Just Walkin' in the Rain" 64
7. What'll You Do Next? 101

Notes 113

Index 121

ACKNOWLEDGMENTS

The trip from idea to finished book wasn't a strange one, but it sure was long. As a result there are many people to whom I am indebted. Many thanks to Rachel Rubin, Jeff Melnick, and Brian Halley at University of Massachusetts Press for their enthusiasm, insight, encouragement, and, perhaps most important, patience. Thanks also to the press's anonymous readers, whose suggestions made this a stronger, more nuanced work. When this book was in its infancy Dale Cockrell was offering invaluable advice and support, something I am glad he still provides. As important in those early days was Arthur Knight, who gave me the analytical tools I needed to become, I hope, a better writer, and Joanne Braxton, whose contributions sharpened my understanding of race and identity.

At Middle Tennessee State University I was fortunate to receive both a Faculty Research and Creative Activity grant and a Non-Instructional Assignment grant, both of which provided me with much-needed uninterrupted research and writing time. I am also extremely lucky to have an incredible archive like MTSU's Center for Popular Music literally downstairs from my office, something I try never to take for granted. The Tennessee State Library and Archives allowed me to peruse box after box of Frank Clement's papers; their vast holdings were a crucial part of my research. I'm grateful for the support of my colleagues in the Department of Recording Industry, especially my brothers in popular music studies Mike Alleyne and Paul Fischer.

Although this sentiment is perhaps too often expressed, there is not a trace of hyperbole when I say that this book would never have been possible without the help of Cass Paley. As I was preparing to publish my first essay on the Prisonaires, Cass called me out of the blue to ask if I'd be willing to be interviewed for a documentary he was making on the group. He then graciously shared with me enormously important information, including interviews with prominent figures in the story. Without his help I wouldn't have written the book.

Many people along the way offered advice, encouragement, and suggestions, read parts of the manuscript at various stages, and sent me newspaper clippings and recordings and in myriad ways helped make the rough places smooth: Jonathan Clark, Colin Escott, Peter Guralnick, Eric Leblanc, Greil Marcus, and Gena Caponi-Tabery. My thanks to Rip Lhamon, from whom I've learned so much, and, as always, to Tom Shea, for getting me started. Also, much appreciation to Don Letts and Handsome Dick Manitoba for being great DJs. Sadly, there are those not here that I wish were: David Sanjek and Stephen Wing, gone too soon, both of whom, at different points in my life, were friends and teachers.

It is with boundless love that I thank my wife, Carol, and son, Eamon, whose confidence that I would finish this project never wavered, even when mine did. No writer could ask for a more supportive family. I couldn't have done it without you.

Jail Guitar Doors, founded by the singer/songwriter/activist Billy Bragg in 2007, is an independent initiative that provides instruments to those who are using music as a means of achieving the rehabilitation of prison inmates. You can support their important work by visiting them at jailguitardoors.org.uk or the U.S. chapter at jailguitardoors.org.

The Mistakes of Yesterday, the Hopes of Tomorrow

PROLOGUE

Poor Old Johnnie Ray

What music does (all music) is put into play a sense of identity that may or may not fit the way we are placed by other social forces. . . . [Music] can also suggest that our social circumstances are not immutable and that other people—performers, fans—share our dissatisfaction.

—Simon Frith, *Performing Rites*

Johnnie Ray needed a hit. His last single, "Johnnie's Coming Home," had managed to scrape the bottom of *Billboard*'s Top 100 singles chart only to vanish within a week. Not helping matters was that America was firmly ensconced in the post-Elvis era, and rock and roll, for anyone still harboring doubts, was for real. A seismic cultural shift that made Ray's heavily orchestrated middle-of-the-road (MOR) pop as well his overblown, stagey vocal style, which had earned him the sobriquet the Prince of Wails, sound pejoratively old school. To return to chart prominence and make a case for his continued relevance as one of pop music's most revered pre-rock vocalists were among the challenges facing Ray and his producer, the Columbia Records majordomo and noted hater of rock and roll Mitch Miller ("It's not music," he famously quipped, "it's a disease"), as they entered Radio Recorders Studios in Hollywood on June 29, 1956.[1]

Born on the Fourth of July 1911 in Rochester, New York, Miller was a graduate of the Eastman School of Music and an accomplished oboist who, after a stint with the Rochester Philharmonic and CBS Symphony, joined the Artist and Repertoire (A&R) Department at Mercury Records in 1948. Within a year he had a chart-topping hit with "That

Lucky Old Sun," recorded by Frankie Laine. In 1950 Miller was hired by the chief executive officer of Columbia Records and a fellow Eastman alum Goddard Lieberson as head of A&R and proceeded to oversee hits for Tony Bennett, Rosemary Clooney, Johnny Mathis, and Doris Day. During this run of success Miller "[defined] American popular music in the postwar, pre-rock era, carefully matching singers with songs and choosing often unorthodox but almost always-catchy instrumental accompaniment."[2]

Despite his gimmicky, if not downright corny, approach to pop music, Miller initially weathered the changes wrought by rock and roll and became widely known to a generation of baby boomers (and their parents) through his multi-million-selling "Mitch Miller and the Gang" recordings and as the genial, goateed host of the gimmicky, downright corny television program "Sing Along with Mitch," which aired on NBC from 1961 to 1964. Later in his career Miller shifted his focus to Broadway, producing musicals with limited success, and he spent his later years, almost until his death in 2010 at the age of ninety-nine, as a symphony orchestra guest conductor.[3]

The idea for Johnnie Ray to record "Just Walkin' in the Rain" was Miller's. Convinced this song could resuscitate his flagging career, Miller had been on Ray's case to record it for nearly two years. In an exhausting daylong session, Ray cut "Look Homeward Angel," "In the Candlelight," "Weaker Than Wise" (a perfectly titled summation of his career), and "If I Had You." He was pleased with the results, but Miller insisted he try "Just Walkin' in the Rain." "I was tired and almost refused to record the song," Ray recalled nearly thirty years later. "I said, 'Mitch, I'm tired. Let's skip this piece of crap.' He said to me, 'John, this could be the song that'll do it for you. Try it. Give it your best shot.' So we did it in two takes, because it was easy, there was nothing to it."[4]

The arranger Ray Conniff ran the session. Miller had brought Conniff to Columbia in the early 1950s as a chief engineer to work with the trumpeter and bandleader Harry James. In October 1955 his arrangement of "Band of Gold," a hit for the professional golfer turned pop singer Don Cherry, defined the Conniff sound: "Meticulous, uptempo pop [with a] regimented beat [and a] chilly innocence."[5] His production work for, among others, Mathis, Laine, and Bennett as well as his solo recordings quickly transformed him into the undisputed king of melodramatic anti-rock pop. Whatever the song or genre, with Conniff in charge the end result would be commercially successful MOR cheese: hokey emotionalism wrapped in a suffocating down of strings, blatting horns, wooden rhythms, and insufferably intrusive backing vocals.

The "piece of crap" Ray reluctantly recorded was in fact a transcendent R&B song that, three years earlier, had profoundly altered the lives of the men who had originally recorded it: John "Junior" Drue, William Stewart, Ed Thurman, Marcel Sanders, and the lead singer Johnny Bragg, collectively known as the Prisonaires, all of them serving time for various offenses at the Tennessee State Penitentiary in Nashville. Early on the morning of June 1, 1953, in the company of an armed guard and prison trusty, the group boarded a bus to make the nearly two-hundred-mile trip from Nashville to Memphis to record "Just Walkin' in the Rain" and "Baby Please" for Sam Phillips at Sun Studios. Prior to working with the Prisonaires, Phillips had recorded some popular R&B songs that included "Rocket 88" by Jackie Brenston and His Delta Cats and "Bear Cat" by the estimable Rufus Thomas, and he was only a year away from releasing Elvis Presley's first singles and forever changing the face of American popular culture. The two songs were finished in a ten-hour session and, while Phillips insisted that "Baby Please" was going to be huge, it was the single's B-side, "Just Walkin' in the Rain," that became the hit. Released on July 8, 1953, it sold in excess of thirty thousand copies in its first six weeks, making it one of the best-selling records of Sun's pre-Elvis era. According to Elvis's biographer Peter Guralnick, "Just Walkin' in the Rain" likely was the record that captured the attention of the young Presley as he read about the studio, the record label, and Phillips, a man who had "staked his reputation on a recording by an unknown singing group and a song whose plaintive notes Elvis heard reverberating over and over in his mind and in his memory and on the air."[6] (So indelible was the impression Bragg's singing made on Elvis that, after his discharge from the army in 1961, Elvis visited him in prison and offered to pay his legal bills. Johnny declined, telling Elvis he would be out in a matter of months. He was released six years later.)

Soon after the record was released the Prisonaires were featured in the pages of the Memphis *Commercial Appeal* and its rival the *Press-Scimitar,* in Nashville's two daily newspapers, the *Tennessean* and the *Banner,* and in the African American magazine of record, *Ebony.* With the help of the penitentiary warden James Edwards and Tennessee's young, progressive governor, Frank Clement, the group made numerous personal appearances throughout Tennessee, all under the watchful eyes of armed guards, and never once attempted to escape.

A melancholy rumination on the end of a love affair, "Just Walkin' in the Rain" was written by Bragg and his fellow inmate, the nonsinging "sixth Prisonaire," Robert Riley. The Prisonaires' recording foregrounds the conversational intimacy of Bragg's croon, gracefully supported by the group's airtight harmonies and Stewart's elegant guitar playing. The tempo is slow but never drags, and the song's climactic moment, Bragg's swooping, ethereal falsetto in the final verse, is breathtaking, a haunting reflection of what the music historian Colin Escott calls "the darkness within him."[7] As vocal performances go, it is sublime, on a par with seminal pop–R&B songs and singers like "If I Didn't Care" by the Ink Spots' Bill Kenny and "It's Too Soon to Know" by the Orioles' Sonny Til.

Ray's version, on the other hand, reveals a puzzling interpretive strategy on the part of Miller and Conniff, suggesting that neither one of them had actually listened to the Prisonaires recording or, if they had, were convinced they could create a more polished, sophisticated facsimile. Ray was best known for his lachrymose ballad singing, and it seemed this song, suffused with sadness and heartache, would be perfect for his teary emoting, considering he, like Bragg, had cut his teeth singing in church and was influenced by a host of black pop, gospel, and R&B singers. Originally signed to Columbia Records' "race label" Okeh in 1950, Ray was so indebted to African American sacred and secular singing that he wrote an article for *Ebony* magazine entitled "Negroes Taught Me to Sing: Famous Crooner Tells What the Blues Taught Him." Try as he might, however, to convey what he had learned from the blues, Ray was simply no match for the heavy hand of Conniff, who buried the song's plangent sentiments under a pile of clutter.

Conniff's arrangement is more up-tempo and inexplicably cheery. Moreover, in a decision bordering on the surreal, Jimmy Duane was brought in to whistle the main melody, reestablishing a mood best described as being jaunty and carefree. Ray's big, vibrato-laden voice belts out the song's title, overenunciating every syllable, attacking each word like a vocal pugilist. A strummed banjo picks up the rhythm, and at the song's bridge, in a quintessentially Conniffian moment, male backup singers punctuate each line with the hushed repetition of the word "walkin'." Ray's vocal gives way to Duane's whistling solo, and the song modulates, lumbering into its final verse and chorus. If it were prose it would justifiably be described as prolix.

Over Ray's strenuous objections, his cover of "Just Walkin' in the Rain" was released in late August 1956 and became the hit Miller had predicted. Reaching #2 on the *Billboard* Top 100 (only Elvis's "Love Me Tender" kept it from reaching #1) as well as spending two months at #1 on the UK Top 20, the record stayed on the U.S. charts for a total of twenty-eight weeks and sold two million copies. Ray's success would earn Bragg nearly ten thousand dollars, his share of the publishing royalties as the song's cowriter. For years his royalty checks arrived at the state penitentiary, his home since 1943.

By the time Ray's version of "Just Walkin' in the Rain" was released, the Prisonaires were, to all intents and purposes, finished. The group was still performing and, more important, still in prison, but the original members Sanders, Drue, and Thurman had been paroled, and Phillips, the group's early booster and producer, made a business decision to largely move Sun Records away from the blues and R&B that had established it for the rockabilly sound of the post-Elvis era. From June 1953 to the winter of 1954 the Prisonaires recorded twenty-two tracks for Phillips, many of them unreleased until 1990. Consigned to the margins of early rock and roll history, the Prisonaires were relegated to novelty status, another of the genre's odd, interesting bits of trivia.

But the story of the Prisonaires and of "Just Walkin' in the Rain" is much more than weightless musical minutiae. With its images of imprisoned African American men singing as a way of restoring their dignity and attaining a modicum of freedom, and the use of music as a path to psychic survival and cultural representation, this is a story of how popular music can be empowering when it is given shape in the most inhospitable of environments and when one considers the impact such an environment has on a song's meaning. It is also a story about the changing cultural geography and musical landscape of Nashville—the Athens of the South, the Buckle of the Bible Belt, and Music City, USA—a city at once struggling with the enormous emotional and physical damage wreaked by Jim Crow racism while fully embracing the postbellum modernist impulse that had guided its political leaders since the city's centennial in 1880, a group that included Governor Clement.

Elected the nation's youngest governor in 1952, Clement embodied this political and cultural duality, honoring the region's particular indigenous traditions yet mindful of the fundamental changes that the South and all of America would experience in the post–Second World War era. Had he lost the governor's race and not been able to make his friend James Edwards the new, reform-minded warden at the penitentiary, the Prisonaires' story would have been one of speculation and myth, there would have been no performances outside the prison and certainly no recording session in Memphis with Phillips. And while it is difficult to argue against the good intentions of Clement and Edwards in allowing the group a certain limited freedom that came with their sudden celebrity status, the use of the Prisonaires as representative of the possibilities of prison reform was ultimately disingenuous and naive. Because the state penitentiary employed a modern variant of the nineteenth-century Auburn system of prison management, which stressed teaching inmates work skills and reduced the burden placed on taxpayers by making prisons more self-sufficient, it was assumed that the success of "Just Walkin' in the Rain" would guarantee the Prisonaires an equally successful postparole career as entertainers. What that assessment neglected to consider was that the group's members were incarcerated for a variety of offenses and were not all eligible for parole at the same time and, perhaps most cruelly, the reality that their marketability was inextricably linked to their lives as inmates. In the end, with the exception of Bragg and the songwriter Riley, there was no musical career waiting for them on the outside.

Even with an ally as dynamic as Phillips the Prisonaires' story lasted a little more than a year, beginning and ending with "Just Walkin' in the Rain." Bragg led the group through a series of iterations, none of them as successful, none of them recording anything as indelible as their only hit, the hit that reanimated Ray's career. In *The Souls of Black Folk*, W. E. B. Du Bois refers to the beauty of spiritual singing as the music sung by the "children of disappointment."[8] Though not spiritual music per se, the music of the Prisonaires, especially "Just Walkin' in the Rain," for all of its triumphs, reflects the disappointment of men caught in a paradoxical search for personal independence while fully cognizant of a future consigned to prison. It is music made by men who, despite their situation, remained hopeful. Their brief career and the unusual circumstances under which it flourished articulate what it means to create music in a hostile, controlled environment and the emotions so deeply embedded in a song—expressions of passion, dignity, and, ultimately, freedom.

CHAPTER ONE

Nashville

To be a poor man is hard, but to be a poor race in a land of dollars is the very bottom of hardship.

—W. E. B. Du Bois, *The Souls of Black Folk*

The year 1880 was one of celebration in Nashville. The city was one hundred years old and poised on the brink of its first period of rapid economic and industrial growth, developments that would last until 1915 and cement its status as a thriving, modern southern city. In his Centennial address Mayor Thomas Kercheval documented in somewhat flamboyant prose the city's growth: "The tangled jungles once the covert of wild beasts and wild men are now the homes of the teeming and busy population. The shriek of the locomotive and the hum of industry is heard instead of the howl of the wolf and the whoop of the red man." This sentiment was in keeping with Nashvillians' "buoyant vision of the city's place in a New South eager to join the national march of progress."[1]

The one-hundred-gun salute that signaled the opening of the Centennial on April 24 also announced the start of urban expansion that would see the city grow from a multiracial, multiethnic cluster of rich and poor numbering just over forty-three thousand to a modern, segmented city of over one hundred thousand by 1915, a city with "clearly defined residential and commercial zones with neighborhoods segregated by race, ethnicity, and social class far more than had been possible before."[2] As was happening in other medium-sized cities at this time, rapid growth and its attendant patchwork of neighborhoods were trapping the city in a paradox of increasing community interdependence and segregation.

In Nashville's centennial year African Americans accounted for nearly 40 percent of the city's population.[3] In the post-Reconstruction era Nashville became a commercial and wholesale agricultural hub for tobacco, corn, cotton, and livestock and, owing to the city's boom economy, experienced a steady stream of black migration.[4] By the thousands African Americans were rejecting rural sharecropping and tenant farming for higher paying jobs as unskilled and semiskilled factory workers working in slaughterhouses, flour mills, fertilizer plants, lumber mills, and iron foundries or as day laborers and domestic servants. These were the "negro jobs," a euphemism that for women meant employment as live-in domestics and for men any type of factory work too dangerous or low paying for whites. Still, for many African Americans, some manumitted for less than twenty years, late nineteenth-century Nashville promised economic security, relative freedom, and the restoration of dignity.[5]

The relative prosperity offered by the city's industrial infrastructure and the rise in the black population led to a worsening of race relations. Working-class whites, threatened by the increased competition for jobs and fearful that increased participation by blacks would lead to lower wages, actively pursued the political disenfranchisement of blacks. Using racist sentiments to frame its ideology, the Democrats defeated the incumbent Republican mayor Kercheval in 1883, interrupting a fifteen-year period of Republican domination in which African Americans were elected to the city council. Given a white population politically motivated by racist-inspired fears of possible economic displacement, interracial relationships, and the spread of communicable diseases, Kercheval's defeat signaled that, as it entered the twentieth century, race relations in Nashville would never be the same. And with the construction of the city's mass transit system in the 1890s, suburbanization and neighborhood segregation were, to those who could afford to leave the city's urban core, only a ten-cent trolley ride away.[6]

In the early twentieth century much of Nashville's black population was concentrated on the north side of town. While this was the city's largest black neighborhood, there was still a fair amount of interracial living in white urban and suburban neighborhoods owing to the large number of black domestics living with their employers in basement apartments of carriage houses. A large portion of black Nashville's working poor resided in small neighborhoods scattered within the city's industrial core, many of them little more than squalid, disease-infested slums. Opportunistic white landlords took advantage of the need for housing and constructed cheap, generic, unpainted frame houses, some built beneath railroad trestles, consisting of two or three rooms and no indoor plumbing. In 1920 rents averaged from ten to fifteen dollars per month, an amount that absorbed much of a family's earned income. Many people were forced to take in boarders as well as raise vegetables and small farm animals in an attempt to lessen their need to purchase food. Still, for many newly arrived African Americans this was the only affordable housing in the city, and in the first quarter of the twentieth century Nashville's growing black working class lived in cramped, unhealthy, desperate places with hardscrabble names like Hell's Half Acre and Black Bottom.

Hell's Half Acre, located in the shadow of the capitol building at the northern end of downtown was Nashville's Harlem and offered its predominantly black clientele a tantalizingly illicit triumvirate of gambling, bootleg liquor, and prostitution. Its heart was Cedar Street (now Charlotte Avenue) between Fourth and Fifth Avenues. A commercial center of black Nashville, Cedar Street was where the Acre's uptown rulers frequented clubs like Dave's Place, the Silver Streak, later called the Cotton Club, and the Blackhawk Restaurant for evenings of jazz, whiskey, and women.

Just northwest of Cedar was Crawford Street. Known as the Combat Zone by regulars, it was the city's red light district. Like most jobs in the city, prostitution was segregated, but interracial liaisons could be had for the right price. And for those seeking a short-term tryst it meant negotiating prices with the street's infamous black female brothel owners, including Ruth "Queen of the Hill" Vance, "Lady" Frank, and "Swamp" Lilly Wilson, who was best known for her dubious personal hygiene and vicious attack dogs. The city's center for saturnalia, Crawford Street had it all: clip joints, live sex shows, easy and affordable access to marijuana, cocaine, and heroin, and a thriving numbers racket that funneled money out of the black neighborhoods and into the pockets of white gangsters.[7] It was also a flashpoint for urban violence and almost by itself was responsible for the city's rapidly escalating homicide rate, which, by the mid-1920s, was higher than that of both New York and Chicago. Crawford Street and many of its black-owned businesses disappeared in the mid-1950s, when urban renewal brought the construction of the James Robertson Parkway.

While Cedar and Crawford offered a potent mix of danger and intrigue, most of the city's black working poor lived in Black Bottom. Located just south of Broadway and not far from the mother church of country music, the Ryman Auditorium, Black Bottom "was a neighborhood that moved from being white to black, then from working-class–middle-class black to poor and black."[8] The region got its name not from the racial makeup of the community, but from the fact that, because of its proximity to the Cumberland River, frequent flooding left the area caked with thick, black mud and dotted with large pools of filthy standing water. A sprawling slum of "tarpaper shacks, decaying tenements, and rough speakeasies," Black Bottom by the early 1900s was subject to ongoing efforts by the city to either "reclaim or eradicate" it.[9]

Despite the poverty and squalor of the area, the historian Bobby Lovett notes, "there was a kind of life for the residents of Black Bottom: boat rides and church baptisms on the Cumberland River, picnics in Greenwood Park . . . band concerts, movies in the downtown theaters, [and] dances and house parties." There were a number of black-owned businesses, a city market, an ice cream factory, and an iron foundry. The African Methodist Episcopal Church, the second-oldest in town, was located there, as were the Pearl School, the city's only Negro high school, and, two blocks to the south, Meharry's Hubbard Hospital, Mercy Hospital, and Millie Hale Hospital, the city's black medical complex. Yet during the first quarter of the twentieth century Black Bottom began to decline, becoming Nashville's "most hated slum . . . so resented by elite blacks and reform-minded whites that the city removed the Negro high school . . . [and] by the 1930s the black . . . hospitals no longer existed in the area."[10]

Although Black Bottom was the city's largest African American enclave, by 1930 the black community, which now accounted for slightly less than 30 percent of the population, lived in neighborhoods to the northwest (Cedar Street north to Jefferson Street, between 8th and 28th Avenues), southeast (Edgehill), and southwest (Trimble Bottom and Fairfield-Green). In these communities, in the "speakeasies and dance halls . . . the city's blues and jazz scene flourished."[11] Nashville's blues singers never achieved the fame of their counterparts in Memphis, Atlanta, Birmingham, and Knoxville because of the city's reliance on radio rather than on records and record players. Radios and record players alike were luxury items that taxed the limited budgets of most working-class black families, but because there were no record stores or record-processing plants in Nashville in the mid-twenties people mostly bought radios. By 1925 the *Grand Ole Opry,* then known as the *WSM Barn Dance,* was being broadcast and almost from the start featured the so-called black hillbilly music of its first and, until Charley Pride's emergence in the 1960s, only African American star, the diminutive harmonica virtuoso DeFord Bailey. Less well known black musicians, many of whom were drawn to Nashville to work in the factories, performed on street corners and in front of hotels. Some, like the banjoist Nathan "Ned" Frazier and the fiddler Frank Patterson, were recorded in 1941, not for commercial release but for documentary purposes by the musicologist John Wesley Work III of Fisk University.[12]

This cultural snapshot evokes what the writer and critic Albert Murray has referred to as the entwined, incontestably mulatto nature of American popular music wherein the descendants of white Europeans participated with their black neighbors in mutual, albeit financially inequitable, cultural exchange as far back as the early nineteenth century. "White solidarity," argues the country music historian Bill Malone, "in both a cultural and political sense, depended in large part on the presence of substantial numbers of black people in southern society. But black people were also indispensable elements of southern folk culture, and they made immeasurable contributions to its shaping and tone. The most expressive component of that culture, music, bears the unmistakable imprint of African American style," an unmistakable imprint that includes the black string band tradition of the 1920s and 1930s.[13]

Although the most popular string bands of the twenties and thirties, for example, Charlie Poole and his North Carolina Ramblers and Gid

Tanner and the Skillet Lickers, were white, record companies recorded black string bands playing "in a tradition rooted in the 19th century, an era pre-dating the blues when banjos and fiddles were the predominant instruments, and guitars a rarity."[14] The recording of these bands was, however, a short-lived phenomenon, occurring after Paramount Records, in 1926, released country blues recordings by Blind Lemon Jefferson that were enormously popular. Jefferson's success meant that many of the leading bands and performers, including the Mississippi Sheiks, Lonnie Johnson, who signed with Okeh in 1925, and "Peg Leg" Howell, in order to tap into the commercial zeitgeist, either had to incorporate blues elements into their musical grammar or simply have their music referred to as blues.

The emergence of commercial hillbilly music—the term *country* wasn't used as a genre designation until the 1940s—occurred a little more than three years after the birth of the race music industry in 1920 when Mamie Smith recorded "Crazy Blues." Soon entrepreneurs like the talent scout and record producer Ralph Peer, who coined the expression *race music,* the all-encompassing term for music recorded by and for African Americans, were traveling throughout the South looking for musicians. A furniture store owner in Atlanta named Polk Brockman encouraged Peer to record the local performer "Fiddlin'" John Carson, whom Brockman had seen in a silent film clip. The two songs recorded by Carson, "Little Old Log Cabin in the Lane" and "The Old Hen Cackled and the Rooster's Going to Crow," which Peer thought were "pluperfect awful," were released in 1923 and sold out almost immediately, announcing the start of the early commercial hillbilly music era. Within two years "the game was fully afoot, and dozens of labels had entered the hunt, actively scouring the country, especially the southern states, looking for anybody—black, white, young, old, man, woman, or child—who might be able to sell records."[15] By the late 1920s, when artists like Tom Darby and Jimmie Tarlton, Cliff Carlisle, Jimmie Davis, and, most notably and influentially, Jimmie Rodgers released records, black blues, jazz, and gospel had been liberally added to what was regarded as white southern folk music. A black blues influence is present in Darby's guitar playing and Tarlton's vocals, which have been described as "the greatest infusion of soul usually attributed to black people."[16] Carlisle was known for his skill at what was called yodeling blues, and Davis, the segregationist governor of Louisiana, best known for popularizing "You Are My Sunshine," occasionally recorded with the black blues guitarists from Shreveport Oscar Woods and Ed Shaffer. Even the less-heralded white duo of Austin and Lee Allen from Sewanee, Tennessee, sang the blues so convincingly that one of their recordings from 1927 was mistakenly classified as race music.

As for the native Mississippian Rodgers, the "Singing Brakeman," who worked as a water boy for black construction groups and was an avid buyer of blues and jazz records, Malone notes that he "accumulated maverick blues fragments and work-song stanzas which he eventually incorporated into his own songs." Rodgers also recorded songs written by a prison inmate named Raymond Hall, who was serving a life sentence in the Texas state prison in Huntsville. Hall had sent Rodgers the song "Moonlight and Skies" in 1929 and went on to compose "The Southern Cannonball," "Ninety-Nine Year Blues," "Gambling Polka Dot Blues" and, most notably, "TB Blues," the song that ominously foretold of the disease that would kill Rodgers at the age of thirty-six in 1933. Rodgers's success and public acclaim were unparalleled and "[inspired] an interest in the blues in at least a generation of country musicians."[17]

In 1921 the Nashville theater owner Milton Starr, in partnership with the entrepreneur Charles Turpin of St. Louis, took over the operation of the Theater Owners' Booking Association—TOBA, or "tough on black asses," as it was more commonly called by the performers who worked it—from its founder, Anselmo Barrasso. Established in 1909, TOBA was the nation's largest black theatrical booking chain, and in Nashville the takeover meant that Starr's Bijou Theater for Negroes (formerly the Grand Opera House) would become one of the main venues for black talent, presenting shows by Ethel Waters, Bessie Smith, Ma Rainey, and Mamie Smith. The Bijou's crosstown rival was the Wagon Wheel, which, despite the implied twang of its name, attracted some of the biggest names in jazz, including Fats Waller and the Chick Webb Orchestra featuring Ella Fitzgerald, who, as was common in the Jim Crow South, played "special shows for white people." The same segregationist impulse guided seating arrangements at larger venues like the Hippodrome, where newspaper advertisements for "colored dance" shows by Fletcher Henderson and Louis Armstrong highlighted "reserved sections for white spectators."[18]

While much of the black working class of Nashville enjoyed the numerous diversions of Cedar and Crawford and frequented shows at the Bijou and Wagon Wheel, there was a growing, politically active, reform-minded black middle class and elite that addressed issues of black disenfranchisement. Four black colleges, Roger Williams University, Meharry Medical College, Tennessee Agricultural and Industrial State Normal School (later renamed Tennessee State University), and, most notably, Fisk University, were in operation in Nashville in the early twentieth century, and the city witnessed a major increase in the number of black physicians, lawyers, and teachers, many of whom chose to stay and work in Nashville, cementing the city's burgeoning reputation as the South's Black Athens. Pivotal to the city's reputation as a center for black scholarship was Fisk University. Founded in 1866, Fisk, among whose students was W. E. B. Du Bois, became the intellectual, cultural, and social focal point of the black middle class of the city and a symbol of the pride and aspirations of the black community, manifested in the growth of such civic and social organizations as the Colored Ladies Relief Society, the Colored Masonic Home, and the Nashville Colored Orphanages.[19] Concern for children was especially acute insofar as, from the turn of the century through the Depression, the mortality rate in black working-class communities was nearly 200 percent higher than that of working-class whites. Black boys and girls left school in large numbers and at increasingly younger ages to work as houseboys, newsboys, and laundresses, earning less than half of what could be earned in a factory. This excessive economic pressure forced generation after generation of Nashville's African American youth out of the classroom and into the streets and laundry rooms. In 1929 eighteen hundred black children started first grade, but of this group only fifty-two graduated from high school; by 1940, a mere 10 percent of black males finished high school.[20] For black adolescent males, the majority of them high school dropouts, petty theft became the most expedient means of supplementing the hand-to-mouth wages they earned as houseboys. Not surprisingly, black juvenile delinquency increased dramatically as youth gangs became surrogate families, providing a kind of social organization lacking in homes broken by divorce, desertion, and death.

In 1926 John Gordon Gay, a graduate student in sociology at Vanderbilt University, personalized this scenario in a master's thesis entitled "Negro Dependency and Delinquency in the Southern Community." The purpose of Gay's study was to "show the bearing which the economic and social status of the family . . . has on the delinquency of colored children." The focus of the study was Henry Emerson, a frail, fourteen-year-old black boy who lived with his family in the Capital Hill area of north Nashville. After three unsuccessful attempts to complete fourth grade—school authorities described him as an "incorrigible truant," and a Stanford-Binet test measured his IQ at 73—Henry dropped out of school and was ultimately brought to Juvenile Court charged with truancy and receiving stolen property.[21]

What Gay's research uncovered was a world of socioeconomic desperation commonly faced by Nashville's black underclass. Having no father present, Henry lived with his mother, an infant brother, and an elderly black woman who provided live-in childcare. Henry's mother earned forty dollars a month working as a cook for a wealthy, white suburban family. Gay, writing with barely concealed racialized condescension, describes Henry's home as

> [a] frame structure, unpainted, covered with smoke and dirt. Front door has two panels missing and the lock is broken. There are two big rooms opening into each other and this in turn opens into a smaller room used for a kitchen. The inside is always in topsy-turvy condition with dirty clothes lying everywhere. The house has a stuffy smell so characteristic of the Negro home. They have a heater to keep the room warm and a clothesline is stretched across the room full of clothes to be dried. The colored woman used the middle of the room as her sleeping quarters and the bed had very ragged and dirty covers on it.[22]

The neighborhood in which Henry lived provided little solace and comfort. Bordered on the east and west by streetcar lines, which created a boundary between the ramshackle homes of the poor black families and those of more prosperous white wage earners, its dirty, ill-kept streets were lined with "begrimed and dilapidated" houses, front yards strewn with rubbish, and backyards "most conspicuous for their tumble-down privies and outhouses."[23] Gay's analysis of Henry's life exemplified the prevalent methodological model of the time, one that explained the social disorganization of the black working poor as directly attributable to a home life lacking in social ritual, which "is generally capable of introducing regularity in conduct and an appreciation for the worthwhile values in life." Although Gay's conclusion is a "variation on the theme of maladjusted country folk in the city" and did not represent the most balanced view of black life in Nashville in the 1920s, the reality was that hundreds, if not thousands, of Nashville's black youth lived in circumstances almost identical to those of Henry Emerson.[24]

Given this scenario, the rise in poverty and juvenile crime not surprisingly brought a rise in the percentage of juvenile incarceration. According to the Tennessee State Board of Prison Commissioners, in the early twentieth century the percentage of prisoners under the age of twenty was "consistently around one-third of the total prison population," and of this population nearly 80 percent were black.[25] As for offenders under the age of eighteen, a report from 1910 on the 3,743 inmates entering the state's workhouses and jails shows a juvenile population of 577, a little more than 15 percent. Of these 577 inmates, 83 percent were black. Although laws were passed to limit the number of juveniles sentenced to adult prisons, "large numbers of black youths were still subject to this form of punishment, even after the opening of the juvenile court in 1910."[26]

In spite of these dismal statistics, many white residents, especially in the decade leading up to the Second World War, regarded their city as one of the most racially progressive in the South, an assumption propagated by a lack of information. The facts about juvenile incarceration rates and the desperate living conditions of people like Henry Emerson were measured against the city's active black bourgeoisie, something that, according to the historian Robert Spinney, "skewed statistical analyses and made the lot of local blacks seem better than it was."[27] Spinney argues that the ignorance of whites about the lives of Nashville's African Americans was partly the result of the city's two daily newspapers, the conservative *Banner* and the slightly less conservative *Tennessean,* both of which refused to cover events in the black community. And while it is true that white readers were more likely to read lurid stories about black crime—for example, stories headlined "Negro Wounded in Knife Fight," "Negro Shot over Dice Game," "43 Negro Women Held for Vagrancy (the euphemism for prostitution)"—there were regular columns, like M. C. Chavis's "Activities of Colored People" in the *Banner* and W. H. Shackleford's "Happenings among Colored People" in the *Tennessean,* that focused on the black middle class. But for Henry Emerson and others like him the future was grim, defined by poverty, limited opportunities, and a statistically higher chance of ending up in the state penitentiary.

CHAPTER TWO

The Prisonaires

If you get a jail sentence, / you must be Nashville bound.

—Furry Lewis, "Viola Lee Blues"

In an interview with Cass Paley, Johnny Bragg fondly recalled the singers who made up the Prisonaires: "[They were] a bunch of good guys: Edward Thurman, William Stewart, Marcel Sanders, John Drue; nice people. And they could sing too, good talent. And they loved everybody, they wasn't the type that hated people. They was good guys. Happy go lucky all the time. And we never blew the privilege. We never broke the rules. When we were going out singing all over the state, we always did the right thing. Always."

Edward Lee Thurman (Tenor Vocals)

At the time of his sentencing for first degree murder on August 12, 1940, Edward Lee Thurman had lived his entire twenty-three years in Nashville, dropping out of school in seventh grade to take a job as a cast iron burner for the Tennessee Enamel Company. Despite the hard, frequently dangerous work—his hands and arms were dotted with scars—the money was good, certainly better than what he earned farming. Still, the dangers outweighed the benefits, and in 1936 he was able to land a better-paying (at thirteen dollars a week) and slightly less dangerous job at the Davidson County Chemical Corporation, a fertilizer manufacturer. A steady job with steady pay meant he could propose to his nineteen-year-old girlfriend, Annie Mae Plumber.

Prior to March 7, 1940, Ed Thurman had never even been in trouble, let alone arrested. Things were fine at work, but his personal life, which he characterized as being disorganized, was made worse by Annie Mae's sudden departure early in their marriage. He continued working at the chemical plant, but after clocking out, and with Annie Mae gone, he simply had too much free time, although drinking and gambling helped him get through the hours when he wasn't working. On the night of March 7, Thurman was at a local pool hall drinking whiskey with a group of friends that included one John Will Hardimon. Another friend, Andrew Hunter, asked Thurman if he could borrow fifty cents. Thurman agreed to lend him the money but told Hunter to give him his pistol as collateral. Thurman then went to a nearby grocery store, where he met a coworker who was about to send a young boy to the chemical plant to pick up his paycheck. He suggested the boy could pick up Thurman's check too. Thurman agreed and told the boy to bring it to his house.

A few hours passed, and Thurman, worried that somebody might have mugged the boy and stolen his check, took matters into his own hands and headed out to Davidson County Chemical. On the way he passed Hardimon and another man identified as Hardimon's cousin. No words were exchanged, but Hardimon suddenly hurled a rock in Thurman's direction. Thurman warned him off. Angry and drunk, Hardimon threatened to knock his teeth in. Thurman picked up his check and returned to the grocery store to settle his bill, then went to the pool hall to get his fifty cents back from Turner. Hardimon was waiting there, drunker and more agitated, and, with two of his uncles supplying extra muscle, he was clearly fixing for a fight. As Thurman walked to the back room to meet Turner, Hardimon hurled another rock that sent a rack of pool cues clattering to the floor. As Thurman turned, Hardimon lunged at him with a knife, and Thurman, in self-defense, shot his assailant with Hunter's gun.

John Will Hardimon took two months and three days to die from the bullet wound to his abdomen. Edward Lee Thurman, though clearly not the instigator and having no prior record, was convicted of first degree murder and sentenced to ninety-nine years in prison.

William Stewart (Baritone Vocals and Guitar)

Bennie White beat Robert Lauderdale to death with a fence rail, but that didn't prevent William Stewart from being convicted of first degree murder and sentenced to ninety-nine years at the Tennessee State Penitentiary. The eldest of nine children, Stewart was only eighteen years old when a white jury of "good and lawful men," citizens of Trousdale County, convicted him, Bennie White, and White's brothers Harding and Crawford of "unlawfully, feloniously, willfully, maliciously, deliberately, premeditatedly, and of malice aforethought . . . strike, beat, bruise, wound, kill and murder the said Robert Lauderdale, and did so commit murder in the first degree . . . against the peace and dignity of the state."[1] A ninety-nine-year sentence was the best Stewart could have hoped for. Lauderdale was white, and Stewart's public defender counseled him and the others that, despite being an accessory to the crime and not a participant, entering a guilty plea was the only way to avoid Old Sparky, the inmates' name for the electric chair at the penitentiary. As was common among white juries at the time dealing with accused African Americans, it seemed more expedient to simply convict them all, regardless of their specific roles in the crime.

That Stewart survived prison is miraculous. Born and raised in Hartsville, Tennessee, he'd never been off the family farm. His education ended after eighth grade, when full-time farming work took precedence over school. He was anything but physically imposing and, like Ed Thurman, was described as being soft-spoken and courteous. On December 4, 1940, a little more than three months after Thurman's sentencing, Stewart left the family farm for his first and, it was assumed, last journey to Nashville, a journey that ended at the State Penitentiary.

Robert Stanley Riley (Cowriter of "Just Walkin' in the Rain")

Bad luck and trouble had been Robert Riley's closest allies from as far back as he could remember. Riley's father died when he was six, he'd quit Pearl High School after completing eleventh grade (although he would later claim to have graduated), and he worked intermittently as a low-wage laborer. Voluble and confrontational despite his slight build, he was said by a number of his employers to be dishonest and troublesome. On January 16, 1946, eleven days before his eighteenth birthday, Riley was convicted on five counts of housebreaking and larceny, sentenced to five concurrent terms of three to ten years, and shipped off to the State Training and Agricultural School in Pikeville. Almost from the day he arrived he was branded as incorrigible and was soon transferred to the Brushy Mountain Penitentiary. After three years there he was paroled on March 4, 1949.

Between March and November of that year, Riley made two life-altering decisions. The first was getting his eighteen-year-old girlfriend, Bertha Gore, pregnant. The second was hooking up with James Robert Jones, breaking into three Nashville homes, and stealing property (mostly clothes) valued at six hundred dollars. In December Riley and Jones were arrested, and on January 26, 1950, Riley was again convicted of housebreaking and larceny, that, since he was now a parole violator, carried a ten-to-fifteen-year sentence. Four days after his incarceration he married Bertha, and although his interviewer at the penitentiary recommended he receive "medium custodial care," it was noted, "A successful social adjustment when he is released from this institution is not anticipated."[2]

John Edward "Junior" Drue (Tenor Vocals)

Most everybody who knew John Edward Drue called him Junior. There was a John Edward Drue Sr., but he'd long been out of the parenting picture after divorcing Junior's mom, Willie Mae Eatherly, and moving to Ohio. While it would be generous to characterize the family as thriving and middle-class, the Drues, according to the Wilson County Welfare Department, resided in "one of the better colored residential sections of Lebanon, and had a better than average income for a colored family."[3]

Drue dropped out of Wilson County High School in the ninth grade and, at the age of fifteen, became a chauffer and houseboy to the realtor M. M. Powell of Lebanon, Tennessee. When he turned seventeen in 1942, he left Powell's employ to join the army, emerging from the experience with an honorable discharge, four months of training as a brick mason, and a propensity for alcohol-fueled recklessness. It was the drink that got him in trouble on the evening of July 8, 1948, when his intoxicated brain convinced him that it would be a good idea to break into Marvin Head's Sweet Shop, steal the cash register, and later drive away in Robert Wynne's Willys Jeep station wagon without Wynne's permission. He hadn't gone far before Wilson County police and Tennessee state troopers arrested him and charged him with grand larceny.

Sentenced to three years, Drue was paroled on August 17, 1950. Two months later, his judgment again compromised by alcohol, he took a 1940 Mercury from the lot of Wilson County Motors for what turned into a two-hour joy ride. Although he returned the car undamaged, he was arrested and charged again with grand larceny. Given his previous conviction for car theft, Drue's counsel advised him to plead guilty. He did, and on January 3, 1951, he began serving another three-year stretch. A successful escape attempt came in July, followed by an equally successful recapture, which added another year to his sentence.

Of all the assessment interviews done with the inmates who would join the Prisonaires, Drue's is particularly interesting in that, lacking the same degree of "familial disorganization" and poverty that, according to prison officials, contributed to the others' turn to crime, his relatively stable upbringing, time in the army, skills training, and employment history left the interviewers flummoxed as to why he had become a not very good thief. Booze certainly played a role—the report characterizes him as a habitual drinker—but with a buck-passing finality the conclusion is that Drue "steals because he wants to steal" and that "it is not probable that he will adjust himself to society when released." Buried under the mountain of sociological cant in the report are two sentences that provide crucial insight into the real Junior Drue: "Reads anything he can get"; the second, more tellingly, notes, "Enjoys all kinds of music."[4]

Marcel Sanders (Bass Vocals)

Marcel Sanders's journey to the Tennessee State Penitentiary began in Chattanooga in 1924. Growing up in a "very poor, disorganized family background,"[5] the youngest and only son of Lucy Green's and Fred Sanders's four children, Marcel and his three sisters were raised by a paternal aunt after Fred was sent to the penitentiary for killing Lucy not long after Marcel was born. After dropping out of Booker T. Washington High School in tenth grade, Marcel joined the navy, but two troubled years as a steward yielded only a bad conduct discharge. Returning to Chattanooga, he worked as a short order cook and was described by his employer as being a fairly intelligent but troublesome employee.

While there is no record as to the nature of the relationship between Marcel Sanders and Margaret Ruth Nix, it is safe to assume that, given his turbulent personal history, it was tempestuous. What prompted the confrontation of March 18, 1949, is unknown, but it ended with Sanders attacking Nix at knifepoint. And in an eerie, inexact, if not entirely unexpected moment of déjà vu, Marcel Sanders followed in his father's footsteps, sentenced to one to five years in the Tennessee State Penitentiary for assaulting Nix with intent to commit involuntary manslaughter.

A little more than a year later, Sanders had been paroled and was back in Chattanooga working as a houseboy and chauffeur for a wealthy white man by the name of Walter Hart. But trouble seemed to stalk the hot-tempered Sanders, and on June 4, 1951, he found himself in another bad situation. A woman by the name of Leola Lake was involved, but this time Sanders was her protector. While Sanders was spending the evening with Lake and her daughter at Lake's home, Ezell Holloway, possibly a jealous ex-boyfriend, showed up in an extremely agitated state and without warning attacked Lake and her daughter with a knife, inflicting serious, if not life threatening, wounds. Sanders drew his knife and lunged at Holloway's neck. He stuck him but wasn't sure it was a good hit, as Holloway ran from the house. He didn't get far. Sanders's blade had severed the jugular vein. Holloway bled to death in the front yard.

Sanders pleaded guilty to one count of involuntary manslaughter. Despite the court's agreeing that he had acted in self-defense, he was convicted of violating the conditions of his parole and on September 15, 1952 was sentenced to one to five years. In an interview with prison officials upon his return, Sanders seems to be a courteous, cooperative, but deeply troubled twenty-seven-year-old who, despite having to serve a short sentence, had little to look forward to upon release. "Close custodial care is recommended," reads his inmate summary, which concludes with the gloomy forecast, "Prognosis when released poor."[6]

John Henry Bragg (Tenor Lead Vocals)

> *The unremitting system of slavery made its subjects not merely idealists who created a sacred universe which promised change and triumph, allowed them to reach back to relive the victories of the past, and drew them into the rich future where the justice and goodness that had been experienced before would exist again; it also made them realists who understood the world as it operated in the present.*—Lawrence Levine, *Black Culture and Black Consciousness*

> *People mess things up, forget and remember all the wrong things. What's left is fiction.*—Daniel Wallace, *Big Fish*

> *I just want to be remembered.*—Johnny Bragg

In African American folklore there are numerous tales involving a trickster named John. In his essay "Negro Folk Expression" Sterling Brown writes that during slavery John always managed to outwit "the devil, the Ole Marster, Ole Miss, and the 'patterollers.'"[7] Postslavery iterations of the trickster John have him going up against racist thugs, greedy landlords, and the police. Lawrence Levine notes that this lore cycle "[was] based upon the kinds of incidents related in these factual and pseudofactual tales, but by removing them from the realm of the immediately personal it allowed storytellers even more scope for their imaginations and their psychic needs."[8] Victory of the oppressed and weak over the powerful and strong is the trope animating these folktales, and for slaves these tales become a "central feature of their consciousness."

The story of John Henry Bragg contains many moments that create a sacred universe promising change and triumph. His biography is a morass of semiapocryphal stories, self-aggrandizement, and undocumented facts. To dismiss him as a liar is to ignore a larger and more significant point: the supposed lies are part of a lifetime of redemption and recovery, the efforts of a man compelled to reclaim a life he feels was twice stolen—once by the criminal justice system and again by the music industry. "Every tongue got to confess," Zora Neale Hurston once wrote, and the confessions of Johnny Bragg, no matter how chimerical, reveal a deep-seated urgency to be heard, respected, and remembered, part of his lifelong battle against contemporary variants of the Ole Marster, Ole Miss, and the patterollers.

Fittingly, the confusion surrounding his life begins at birth. Depending on whom you believe, John Henry Bragg was born on February 26, 1925, January 18, February 8, May 6, or May 18, 1926. The second date is the official one, having been reported in the Davidson County census of 1930, while the third is the one recorded by the Tennessee State Penitentiary and the fourth is the most dramatic, as it means his sentencing occurred on the day of his seventeenth birthday. John Henry was born to Wade and Maybelle Bragg, most likely in 1926, the year that the Vanderbilt student John Gordon Gay completed his study of Henry Emerson and Nashville's black working class. Johnny's home life wasn't terribly different from Henry's. He lived in a cramped, rundown house on Herman Street, just off Jefferson in north Nashville. He was the fourth child in six years—there had been two boys, James and Wade Jr., and a daughter, Dorothy—but Johnny's birth was complicated, and Maybelle did not live to see her new son. For the grieving Wade, giving up work to raise his children was out of the question, as the family relied on the six dollars a week he earned working twelve-hour shifts for the Nashville, Chattanooga and St. Louis Railway. While Wade worked, Maybelle's mother, Parthenia, who lived across the street, provided his childcare needs.

As if being an elderly single woman raising four children wasn't hard enough, exacerbating the situation were Johnny's special needs—he had been born blind. Unsurprisingly, there is scant evidence for what caused his sightlessness (though the doctors told Wade it was permanent) and the circumstances surrounding his miraculous recovery. Johnny's telling is decidedly blasé, as if he knew all along his sight would return: "Maybe I used to know [what happened], but I forgot. I would just say that [my vision] cleared up." A similar insouciance marks his recollection of how old he was when his vision began to return: "Doggone if I know. Maybe I was three, four, five, something like that." The blind black child liked to sing and was a hit with the doctors, who were fond of his rendition of the crooner Gene Austin's "My Blue Heaven" and the minstrel song composed by Drew Sterling and Harry Von Tilzer in 1905, "What You Going To Do When the Rent Man Comes Round? (Rufus Rastus Johnson Brown)"[9]

Johnny spent three years at Parthenia's. She was simply too old to adequately take care of four children, especially one who was blind, but Johnny always spoke fondly of her and of the hours he spent listening to her player piano. That Parthenia had such an item in her home was a fortuitous luxury. A player piano was an expensive piece of musical furniture, costing around six hundred dollars, and was not usually found in working-class homes. For a while the children lived with Wade's sister Mattie and brother-in-law Augustus Haines, a Baptist minister. It was 1939 before Wade, now remarried to a woman named Mary Etta, was able to bring his family back together by securing one of the units at Andrew Jackson Courts near Fisk University, the first public housing project for African Americans in Nashville.

By the time the family moved into Andrew Jackson Courts, Johnny had completed the sixth grade, but he dropped out of school at that point and was regularly getting into trouble. At first it was petty theft—at thirteen he was picked up for stealing soft drinks off a delivery truck—but soon escalated to the occasional house break-in, culminating in a three-block joyride in a stolen car that he swears he didn't know was stolen. That landed him inside the Tennessee State Training and Agricultural School in Pikeville for a month. Upon his release from Pikeville, he spent much of his time on the streets of north Nashville, and when he wasn't stealing things he was singing with a group of what he called "little young street guys" informally known as the Black Legion.[10] Johnny's considerable vocal skills allowed him to assume the role of lead singer in these makeshift groups. The material leaned heavily on gospel, like the Reverend Thomas Dorsey's "Precious Lord," an audience favorite, along with pop songs he'd learned from Parthenia's player piano.

Then came the imprimatur of none other than Billie Holiday. Johnny's chance meeting with her occurred backstage at the Silver Streak

Club when, according to Johnny, he was eleven. As Johnny tells it, the owners used to let him in to collect empty soda and whiskey bottles; the small amount of cash he got for redeeming the glass he used to go to the movies. One evening an irritated Cab Calloway chased the kid out of his dressing room and into Holiday's. Seizing the moment, Johnny informed her of his intention to be a singer. "She said, 'Let me hear something,'" he remembers. "I said I could sing 'A Tisket A Tasket,' she said, 'You can sing!' I'll never forget that, she was a good lady, but she wasn't nothing to play with."[11]

While fascinating and, if true, certainly life changing, what makes this moment potentially apocryphal is that it lacks enough hard evidence to be entirely credible. If dates mean anything in this story, Johnny's claim to being eleven at the time places this fortuitous meeting in 1937. Holiday would have been twenty-two, four years into a career that began when she met the jazz critic and entrepreneur John Hammond in Harlem. Hardly an unknown at the time, she'd already sung with Benny Goodman's band, appeared in the film *Rhapsody in Black,* recorded with a small combo led by the pianist and Goodman protégé Teddy Wilson, and hooked up with her most sympathetic musical partner, Lester Young.[12] Had Holiday appeared in Nashville in 1937, it probably would have been as a singer in Count Basie's band, which also featured the vocalist Jimmy Rushing. In Johnny's story, Basie goes unmentioned and is replaced by Cab Calloway. Residing, as do many of Johnny's stories, in a hazy purgatory of verisimilitude, his encounter with Lady Day, whether real or imagined, is part of a larger authenticating strategy wherein his talent, which has never been in dispute, needs to be recognized and validated by a famous artist. The strategy enables him to simultaneously strengthen his individual greatness while reaffirming his role in popular music history. Such is the difference between actual truth and imaginative truth, the difference between a life lived and a more compelling facsimile in which, once sharing the company of legends, Johnny elevates himself from a place far below the horizon of recognition and directly into the heart of the narrative.

Able to eke out an existence by singing, hustling, and occasionally stealing, Johnny needed to find a less erratic means of earning a living.

At sixteen he took a job common among black adolescents with little formal education, working as a houseboy and chauffer for a Mrs. H. B. Whiteman (on some documents her name is spelled Wightman), who resided in the affluent neighborhood of Belle Meade. Johnny added the chauffer part. Mrs. Whiteman claimed that while she found him to be a very nice boy who did his chores, mostly yardwork, satisfactorily, he was never allowed to drive the car. After nine months she had no more work for him.

Johnny's inmate file at the Tennessee Department of Corrections reads as follows: "Subject's version of the offense: Was charged with having raped six colored girls at different times in the night on the streets of north Nashville. Subject denies having attacked any of the girls." Johnny says it was his girlfriend, Jenny Price, who got him in trouble, trouble so deep he would likely spend the rest of his life in jail. Of all his recollections, the circumstances leading to his incarceration require little embellishment. It was a nightmarish conflation of false accusations, aggressive prosecution, inadequate, if not downright apathetic, defense, and racism. He was still a child, a juvenile offender, but he was tried as an adult, and from the moment he was arrested he never had a chance of getting anything remotely resembling a fair trial.

Johnny caught Jenny in bed with his friend Chester. Heated words quickly turned into a physical confrontation, with Johnny getting the worst of it, especially from Jenny. Perhaps Jenny had her liaison with Chester out of spite. For one salient fact Johnny always left out when telling this story was that he was already married, to a woman named Celene Nickelson. They'd tied the knot in 1942, when both were sixteen, and at the time of Johnny's sentencing she was still living with his father, Wade. When the fight with Chester and Jenny was over, Johnny was bloodied, bruised, and humiliated, but he never imagined that Jenny's accusations of rape would be taken seriously. Steadfastly maintaining his innocence, Johnny has always believed that what began as a domestic dispute turned into a frame-up by racist members of Nashville's all-white police force who saw him as a convenient fall guy to take the rap for a half dozen unsolved sexual assaults of black women. One detective in particular, surnamed Ruby, was, according to Johnny, the principal investigator in the case, and he coerced testimony and "positive identification" from the six women in question. The Bragg family did receive some good news: Jenny recanted her statement, and her family dropped the charges, but it was too little too late, and Johnny was charged with six counts of rape.

Case number 37509, *State of Tennessee v. John Henry Bragg,* was heard before an all-white, all-male jury in the Davidson County Criminal Court, Judge Charles Gilbert presiding. Assistant Attorney General John C. Askew Jr. had compiled an impressive list of thirty-one witnesses, including Detective Ruby, testifying for the state. Johnny pleaded not guilty and was told by his public defender to either remain silent or risk a death sentence: "[My lawyer] told my daddy 'He might go to the electric chair, just let me handle [it] like I want to handle [it] and we'll have him out in nine months.'"[13] His lawyer was right in that he did avoid the electric chair, but a nine-month sentence proved wildly optimistic. The jury found Johnny guilty on all counts, and on May 6, 1943, Judge Gilbert sentenced him to six concurrent terms of ninety-nine years. "Man Gets 99 Years for Criminal Assaults," read the headline in the *Banner;* "18-Year-Old Negro Sentenced to 99 Years," reported the *Tennessean.* The stories were little more than a couple of tersely worded paragraphs; few readers noticed, even fewer cared. With a similar matter-of-factness his Department of Corrections inmate summary concludes, "This is a negro, 17 years of age, 5'7" tall, weighing 150 pounds. He reported a sixth grade education, close family ties and has been geographically stable. He rationalizes his troubles in terms of innocence and stated he could not understand why the six colored girls identified him as being their attacker. Close custodial care is recommended in this case."

In accordance with sentencing guidelines, John Henry Bragg would become eligible for parole on October 29, 1976.

CHAPTER THREE

The Prison, the Governor, and the Warden

Prison has everything the free world has. There's commerce in prison. There's sex in prison. There's love in prison. And there's art.

—Steve Earle

The Tennessee State Penitentiary, the state's first prison, opened in Nashville in 1831. Previously, offenders had been housed in county jails, and although the idea of a state prison system seemed like a good idea, it wasn't long before the facility had outlived its usefulness. In 1898 the new Main Prison opened in Cockrill Bend in West Nashville. An imposing gothic fortress constructed of Pikeville sandstone and white brick, the new state penitentiary had eight hundred single-occupancy cells measuring six by six by eight feet and latticed doors that maximized light and ventilation. There was no wood in the construction, and, as reported in the newspapers at the time, "It is absolutely impossible for the building to burn." Hailed as one of the nation's first modern prisons, it served the state of Tennessee (although perhaps not its inmates) well until it closed in 1992.[1]

From its earliest days the penitentiary employed, as noted earlier, the reformist Auburn system, a new approach to penology that by the mid- to late nineteenth century was a common form of prison management. The Auburn system, named after the Auburn Penitentiary in upstate New York, where the system was first implemented, was part of the goal of postrevolutionary America of replacing the harsh justice of British tyranny—the stock, whipping posts, and branding irons—with institutions that would punish and reform criminals more humanely. As a system of prison management the Auburn model "was a clear reference to a monastic model; a reference, too, to the discipline of the workshop."[2]

The fundamental brilliance of the system, according to its architects and supporters, was that it was in fact a duplication of society, a society whose moral parameters were rigidly defined by the system's creators. As a result, the system was designed as a microcosm wherein "individuals are isolated in their moral existence, but in which they come together in a strict hierarchical framework, with no lateral relation, communication being possible only in a vertical direction."[3]

Under the Auburn system of incarceration, prisoners shared space only during work time and meal hours, and then in absolute silence. Prisoners could speak only to guards in a low voice and only if they received permission. Those violating the code of silence were punished quickly and cruelly. Inmates were flogged for talking and flogged again if they denied it, punishment that led to the development of an elaborate form of sign language among the inmates that, if discovered by the guards, also resulted in a flogging.[4] The imposition and strict enforcement of the code of silence was to keep prisoners from fomenting insurrection or planning an escape and, in an effort to reform the inmate population, prevented convicts from passing on their crime techniques. Ultimately, the code of silence was an effort to break their spirits, "bringing about a readiness to accept correction . . . [and] force them . . . to reflect on their sins, to repent and resolve ever after and obey the commandments of God."[5]

The use of labor as a means of rehabilitation through moral inculcation was as important to the success of the Auburn system as its implementation of a monastic hierarchy. Penal labor was the vehicle by which violent prisoners, in theory, learned habit, order, and obedience, and in doing so generated enough income for the prison's ultimate goal of economic self-sufficiency. Most nineteenth-century penal theorists agreed that the application of one's physical and mental capacities in a routinized, structured fashion reduced violent tendencies and had an overall calming effect on prisoners. Leon Faucher, writing in 1838, emphatically cut to the heart of the Auburn system, noting that "work is the providence of modern peoples; it replaces morality . . . work must then be the religion of prisons."[6] Auburn prisons set up factories, leased out convict labor to the highest bidder, and for years produced a wide array of products that included nails, shoes, furniture, clocks, wagons, even rifles. Auburn proponents agreed that these new works skills, combined with a reformed attitude, meant paroled convicts would be better able to cope in an increasingly industrialized marketplace.

Louis Dwight, a Yale-educated ordained minister, used the Auburn paradigm in founding the Boston Prison Discipline Society in 1825. Motivated by his goal of saving the souls of wayward men and dedicated to the improvement of public prisons, the Boston Prison Discipline Society, despite its harsh name, used the Auburn model as the basis for prison reform. Dwight's initiatives included individual cells, the distribution of Bibles, a classification system that separated violent criminals from the mentally ill and from youths and children, school programs, and matrons for female prisoners. Most important was Dwight's concern that all prisoners, irrespective of race and gender, be treated with respect and that industries be developed to create profit for the prison through convict labor and to produce a new labor force. Dwight's version of the Auburn model was built upon the premise that "good food, clothing, medical aid, discipline, and economically practical and productive labor reform" would, in the long run, aid in the "reformation of the criminal himself."[7]

Despite these assertions, however, penal labor was not the panacea that supporters of the Auburn system claimed. Prisons, by and large, did not produce a large population of skilled ex-cons with transferable skills suited for an increasingly industrialized marketplace. Penal labor was in fact the creation of power relationships wherein the newly skilled convict-workers were dominated by the prison workshop's goal of producing individuals acclimated to the demands of industrial society. The once-violent criminal, his life now largely filled with mind-numbing, repetitive work, was not taught skills to enhance his opportunity for future employment but was made docile through the process of work and the payment of wages. Remuneration for labor, much lower for convicts that for the general populace, defined the condition of the convict's existence. Payment of wages and attendant feelings of accomplishment resulting from earning one's way were meant to produce the "love and habit" of work in the convict. This version of the Auburn management system would guide the changes made at the Tennessee State Penitentiary during the tenure of Governor Frank Clement and Warden James Edwards and help the Prisonaires achieve their modicum of fame.

During the antebellum era the population of the Tennessee State Penitentiary was predominantly white; African Americans were not sent to prison in large numbers, their criminal offenses (alleged or otherwise) being dealt with locally, swiftly, and brutally. After the Civil War, however, freed blacks represented a threat to southern white supremacy, and the local enforcement of racist-inspired jurisprudence was quickly codified by the state in an attempt by whites to systematically reestablish their dominance.[8] As the historian H. Bruce Franklin notes, "Central to this historical redefinition of the role of black people was an ideological definition of them. No longer were they just a subhuman race; now they were thought of as a race of criminals."[9] Postbellum laws written to criminalize virtually any form of black behavior brought about a dramatic racial shift in the prison population of Tennessee. In 1865 blacks made up 33 percent of the inmate population at the state penitentiary; by 1867 that number had increased to nearly 60 percent; by 1869 it was 64 percent, and it averaged 60 percent well into the twentieth century. These increases were in stark contrast to the black population of the entire state, which was rarely higher than 20 percent.[10]

With the shift in the racial makeup of the prison population came a shift in the attitude toward employment favored by the Auburn system. While much of the infrastructure remained—for example, the strictly enforced hierarchical framework and labor as a way of eliminating violent behavior—the system itself had become racialized. The goal of teaching prisoners habit, order, and obedience remained, but replacing the idea of inculcating inmates with the love and habit of work and of work as the providence of modern peoples were the large profits to be made through convict leasing.

In Tennessee the introduction of convict leasing directly corresponded to the increase of the black inmate population and "more than any other innovation of the time, helped support economic recovery, the maintenance of white dominance, and the conquest of Northern capitalism." The state leased to the highest bidder all or part of the convicts for a fixed sum and transferred to the lessee all the expenses of management, including housing, protection, food, clothing, and guarding, connected with the employment of the prisoners. The lessee was also given complete authority over the control and punishment of the prisoners, relieving the state of all obligation and responsibility, while exposing the prisoner to more violent and potentially life-threatening situations than they faced in prison. Most important, all payments by the lessee were clear profits to the state.[11]

By the 1870s the inmate population had become the principal workers on a $14-million project to rebuild the state's railroads. Coal mining companies regularly leased convict labor and, in a stunning move in 1884, the Tennessee State Coal, Iron and Railway Corporation leased Nashville's entire prison population.[12] It was a bleak existence, and for most convicts leased out the only relief was escape or, more frequently, death. As a result of the convict lease system, thousands of African Americans awoke from "rosy dreams of freedom and forty acres and a mule to find themselves shackled to the task of rebuilding the wealth of the South in hopeless penal slavery."[13] In the early 1940s, when the members of the Prisonaires began entering the Tennessee State Penitentiary, the prison had relied on the Auburn system for over a century. Convict leasing, its intense brutality now a matter of public record, had been abolished in most southern states by the mid-1930s, and prison work for profit returned to the contract model that allowed business to use convicts as a poorly paid, temporary workforce.

But while the brutality of convict leasing had been abolished in theory, it was an ongoing reality within the walls of the Tennessee State Penitentiary, especially during the lengthy tenure of Warden Glenn Swafford. Swafford, a former prison guard, became warden in 1915, the start of a career in prison administration that would see him serve eleven governors. A strict disciplinarian not averse to using violence, fear, and intimidation to control the inmate population, Swafford employed a severe permutation of the Auburn model (more in keeping with its original iteration), and it wasn't long before the penitentiary became known as Swafford's Graveyard.[14]

The idea that Swafford might have allowed the Prisonaires to record and perform outside the penitentiary was unthinkable, and, as one who ran a prison known among its inmates as a graveyard, he acted in a completely predictable way. As far as he was concerned, it was enough that he let them sing and keep radios and record players in their cells. Swafford lacked Edwards's foresight and was decidedly uninterested in fundamentally changing the way the prison ran. He simply refused to accept the attendant risks and negative publicity surrounding special treatment of inmates, regardless of how talented they were.

Accepting the risks that Swafford avoided was a gamble for Edwards but perhaps not completely surprising. He understood that the most expedient method of promoting prison reform to a skeptical public was through media exposure and public appearances—what better way to demonstrate how far these men had come? He may also have been aware that the recording of music made by inmates had been going on for decades before any of the Prisonaires were incarcerated. (Swafford certainly knew this, as for years he had grudgingly let inmates be recorded by folklorists on orders from the governor.) The main difference was that the early recordings were done by folklorists, anthropologists, and sociologists who were interested in documenting and preserving African American vernacular song traditions, not in substantiating arguments for more progressive penology or searching for future pop music stars. The tempestuous Hungarian émigré folklorist Lawrence Gellert, a scholar steeped in radical politics, spent much of his life working in relative obscurity as he recorded songs sung by black work gangs as early as 1924. The sociologist Howard W. Odum, upon receiving doctoral degrees from Clark University in Worcester, Massachusetts, and Columbia University, returned to his native south and, after brief stints teaching at Emory University and the University of Georgia, was named Kenan Professor of Sociology at the University of North Carolina, a position he held until his death in 1954, and began archiving black folk music performances on cylinder recordings.

While teaching at North Carolina, Odum and his coauthor, Guy B. Johnson, published *The Negro and His Songs* in 1925 and, the following year, *Negro Workaday Songs*, two important early studies of African American vernacular music, to emphasize the importance of recordings as a means of documenting and disseminating vernacular music. Although not a folklorist or archivist, David L. Cohn, the son of a slave owner from Greenville, Mississippi, established a writing career after the family's cotton plantation went bankrupt and in his book *Where I Was Born and Raised* (1940), wrote movingly about black folk songs and spirituals.[15]

But of all the folklorists venturing into the Deep South to record the music of imprisoned black men and women, none achieved greater prominence than John Lomax and his son Alan. Though embarking on their odyssey of a decade-plus after Gellert and Odum (as well as after the publication of Dorothy Scarborough's *On the Trail of Negro Folksongs* in 1925 and Newman I. White's *American Negro Folksongs* in 1928), "no one before the Lomaxes," notes John Szwed, "had appreciated the richness of creativity within prison life, and none had sought it out with such dogged persistence." According to Szwed, John Lomax was fascinated by prisons in a manner particular to southern white men who "had grown up hearing stories of men who were broken by heat and dehydration and the dusk-to-dawn work of the prison farms." Southern prison farms, cruelly so, resisted the inevitable onset of industrialization "since they were never short of labor. . . . [For] black men, such prison work meant a return to slavery."[16] Alan regarded prisons as repositories wherein black communal singing traditions, which, he argued, were vanishing in part because of sharecropping, flourished, creating distinctive styles from prison to prison. As he wrote in 1993,

> This vein of African American creativity flourished in the state pens because there it was essential to the spiritual as well as the physical survival of the black prisoners. . . . A new prisoner, confronting the torture of dawn-to-dark toil in the blazing heat, also faced a musical challenge, which helped him endure his first hellish weeks in the pen; he had to learn how to sing with the prison veterans. These hard boys, who rutted, fought, and killed in overcrowded prison dormitories, could sink their differences, feel the black pride and power of their group, and forget the bitter, bitter cares as their choruses rolled across the fields.[17]

Starting in 1933, when Alan was eighteen, and returning regularly until 1947, the peripatetic Lomaxes traveled throughout the South, from Texas (where at Goree State Farm near Huntsville they recorded the brilliant Hattie Ellis) to Louisiana (recording at the state's most notorious prison farms, Angola and Parchman), Mississippi, and Kentucky. On their way back to Washington, D.C., they made a brief stop in Tennessee, where, on their first song-gathering trip, after receiving permission from then-governor Harry Hill McAlister, they recorded inmates at the Memphis Work House and in Nashville at the Tennessee State Penitentiary. It was in Nashville that a prisoner with the intimidating moniker Black Sampson refused the Lomaxes' request to sing secular songs, citing religious reasons (he considered them obscene and blasphemous). He finally acquiesced after being ordered to cooperate by Warden Swafford.[18]

Of all the inmates recorded by the Lomaxes none made a more indelible stamp on American popular music history than Huddie Ledbetter, better known as Lead Belly. Middle-aged by the time the Lomaxes met him in 1933, Lead Belly, like Johnny, had survived a hardscrabble, violent upbringing through a potent combination of bad attitude and indomitable will. Physically intimidating despite his size (while most imagine him to be enormous, at five seven he was a compact, sinewy 170 pounds), he was different from the average Angola inmate: "[Lead Belly] spoke with confidence, pride, and an undisguised intelligence, none of it part of the standard prisoner's repartee. He moved like a boxer, light on his feet, and had the muscles of having been a lead man on the prison work crews for years."[19]

In some ways Johnny's story reflects that of Lead Belly insofar as both men, to varying degrees, sang their way out of prison. Despite working in different genres nominally considered pop music, both men achieved success and were weighed down by the inescapability of having been a convict. Prior to the intercession of the Lomaxes, Lead Belly had already sung his way to freedom, in 1925 while serving a seven-to-thirty-year sentence at the Sugar Land prison in Texas for murder. Governor Pat Neff, in a manner mirroring the relationship between Clement and the Prisonaires, became so enamored of his music that he often brought friends to the prison to hear performances by Lead Belly and other black and white inmates. After Lead Belly had served the seven-year minimum, Neff commuted the remainder of his sentence. Lead Belly landed in Angola in 1930 after he was arrested for assault with intent to kill—he claimed he used a knife in self-defense when he was attacked by three white men—and received a six-to-ten-year sentence. During the Lomaxes second visit to Angola in 1934 they recorded his paean to Governor O. K. Allen in which he asked to be released (a theme the Prisonaires would revisit in a similar recorded tribute to Clement), which he was, one month after the Lomaxes delivered the record to Allen. However, as Szwed notes, "[Lead Belly] was freed [not as a result of the song] but under Louisiana's 'good-time laws' having satisfactorily served four years, five months, and five days of his six- to ten-year sentence."[20]

Allowing inmates any degree of creative expression, as Clement and Edwards would learn, cannot be done without courting controversy and public opprobrium. To those who supported Swafford's harsh version of the Auburn model, a successful reintegration into society required strict adherence to the prison's immutable hierarchy, one that reinforced the idea that a rehabilitated prisoner was one who had learned his place and mastered a transferable skill, a lesson reinforced by regular beatings.

It was one thing to let prisoners sing and be recorded for posterity by archivists—after all, this was ostensibly an academic rather than a commercial exercise—but to permit inmate bands and vocal groups to entertain fellow convicts, release recordings, and, as would happen with the Prisonaires, perform in public seemed an egregious mistake, one that, according to critics, lost sight of the reason the men were behind bars. This assessment, however, discounts the positive impact that performing inside and outside the prison has on participating inmates. One recent study involving prison choirs allowed to perform in public noted that, among the participants, there was a marked improvement in the inmates' "emotional stability, sociability, happiness, and joviality."[21] In 2002, VH-1 aired *Music behind Bars,* an eight-part program on prison music initiatives in the United States. The producer of the series, Arnold Shapiro, in defense of a program he knew would provoke outrage, stated, "[By] showing the redemptive aspect of music in prisons, we would be showing how these music programs take some of the most violent prisoners and make good prisoners out of them.... [T]hat makes it safer for the correctional officers who work inside the prison without weapons as well as the dozens of men and women who go in and out every day: doctors, lawyers, psychologists and the rest."[22] Still, the program drew the ire of both victims' families and the disputatious conservative talk show host Bill O'Reilly, who decried and ridiculed the efforts of the show's creators, noting that one of the featured inmates, the convicted murderer Christopher Bissey, "should be doing hard labor, not playing the drums and having a good time."[23]

American popular music has seen its share of successful performers who have ended up in jail—a list that includes Chuck Berry (twice), James Brown, the late Buddy Miles, David Crosby, the late Gil Scott-Heron, Steve Earle, the guitarist Wayne Kramer of the MC5, and, more recently, Lil Wayne—some of them, like Miles, performing with other inmates in prison bands or phoning in freestyle rhymes, as Lil Wayne did on the track "Light Up" by Drake while serving eight months in Rikers Island for a weapons conviction. Although he never spent more than a couple of nights in jail on misdemeanor charges, Johnny Cash is perhaps best known for his outspokenness on prison conditions and prisoners' rights, memorably articulated in his performances at Folsom and San Quentin prisons.

Arguably the most famous singing ex-con in American popular culture is Vince Everett, the character played by Elvis Presley in the film *Jailhouse Rock* (1957). Imprisoned for beating a man to death while protecting an abused woman, Vince demonstrates his vocal skills at first by singing in his cell and later on in a television broadcast of a prison talent show. After he's paroled, Vince starts his own record label, becomes a rock and roll star, heads to Hollywood to star in movies (the plot has many similarities to Elvis's real life), becomes insufferably egotistical, alienates those closest to him, only to be redeemed after an injury to his larynx jeopardizes his singing career. As Peter Guralnick described it "[*Jailhouse Rock*] offered a neat little parable in black and white on the debilitating effects of fame."[24] What is fascinating about the film is that hardly anyone considers Vince's time in prison an impediment; in fact, in the film's most lavishly choreographed sequence, featuring the title song by Jerry Leiber and Mike Stoller, prison is portrayed as a kind of summer camp for incorrigible truants rather than a maximum security facility for hardcore felons. Like the Prisonaires, Vince doesn't shy away from his time inside, embracing his status as an ex-con as a unique means of marketing and promoting his music.

For every famous performer, real or fictitious, who runs afoul of the law, numerous others are shunted to the margins of pop music history or never have their music heard by anything other than a captive audience. Along with the aforementioned Hattie Ellis there is the Marquette Prison Band, which in 1962 released the single "The Lifer" on Longhorn Records out of Dallas. The song is an autobiographical account of the circumstances leading to the imprisonment of the song's composer, Al Gliva, who was serving a life sentence for second degree murder. In 2007 the British singer-songwriter Billy Bragg started "Jail Guitar Doors" (named after the Clash song), an initiative that provides instruments to inmates as part of their rehabilitation. In addition to producing shows in prisons, the program, which as of 2009 has an American chapter cofounded by Bragg and Wayne Kramer, takes selected inmates on tour to promote its efforts. Six decades after Lead Belly's release from "the bloodiest prison in America," the Canadian blues singer Rita Chiarelli, accompanied by the filmmaker Bruce McDonald, went to Angola to document her performances with many of the prison's longtimers. Released in 2010, *Music from the Big House,* according to its creators, allowed outsiders to witness "remarkable voices of hope as their love of music radiates humanity and redemption on their quest for forgiveness."[25]

The controversy over musical expression among inmates as a component of rehabilitation remains a trope in the ongoing discourse on the philosophy of penology. Allowing creativity to flourish in an inhospitable environment is anathema to those who insist that the purpose of incarceration is to strip away the inmate's humanity and break their will, despite the fact that a number of prison wardens see these moments of expressivity as having nothing but positive benefits. "For [the inmates] it's a way of coping," notes a warden at a maximum-security lockup in rural Maine, "it's a way of expressing themselves and a way of making the time go faster. It reduces the idleness and, as a result, they don't seem to get into so much trouble. I see it as a win-win all around."[26] This seems a reasonable, though not universally accepted, argument in contemporary times, but in the mid-1950s such thinking marked a radical departure in both prison management and inmate rehabilitation. For the members of the Prisonaires, the situation would have been markedly different had Swafford remained in charge. For the group to be heard outside prison walls would require the intercession of a new governor and warden along with an infusion of new political will.

Frank Goad Clement was born in the small, middle-Tennessee town of Dickson in 1920. Growing up in a family that included a great-grandfather, grandfather, and father who worked in state and local politics, Clement, by the age of ten, had fixed his sights on the governor's job. Handsome, charismatic, and gregarious, he was a gifted debater and extemporaneous speaker, personality traits and communication skills honed as a teenager at the Shipp School of Expression, run by his aunt Dockie Shipp Weems. Known throughout the state as the Tennessee Spellbinder, Clement frequently relied on his oratorical proficiency during his campaigns and tenure as governor. After attending his father's alma mater, Cumberland University, for two years, he transferred to Vanderbilt University School of Law, where, as a second-year student, he scored the highest grade on the Tennessee bar exam and was the youngest of the 244 examinees.[27]

Upon graduating from Vanderbilt in 1942, Clement spent a year in the FBI investigating "espionage, sabotage, problems of internal security, selective service investigations, and general criminal investigations." He served in the army from 1943 to 1946, stationed in Georgia and Texas, and, after being discharged, returned to Dickson as general counsel for the Railroad and Public Utilities Commission. It was here that he tied his political fortunes to the Democratic Party as president of both the Dickson County Young Democrats Club and the Young Democrats Clubs of Tennessee, fortuitous political unions that would aid in his rapid rise to prominence. In 1948 Clement served as an alternate delegate-at-large to the Democratic National Convention and the following year was elected state commander of the American Legion. In 1950 he left the Railroad and Public Utilities Commission and reentered the military during the Korean War, where he served as a reserve officer at Camp Gordon in Virginia. That same year, at the age of thirty, he announced his candidacy for governor in the Democratic primary of 1952.[28]

Clement ran on a platform of no new taxes and called for improvements in health care, including mental health, welfare benefits, and education. In a speech he gave in Lebanon, Tennessee, in 1954 Clement expressed what he hoped his legacy would be: "I hope that someday the opening paragraph of a Tennessee history yet to be written will say of my administration: During the humane administration of Frank G. Clement, Democrat from Dickson, from 1953–59, the aged, the needy, the lame and the halt, the blind and the mentally ill citizens of Tennessee were the beneficiaries of unprecedented recognition and advancement. Clement was known as the humane governor." Civil rights, however, an increasingly important issue brought to the fore by the state's educated black middle class and elites, were not part of the debate. Though emblematic of the new breed of southern Democrats, Clement was "watchful and uncommitted" on desegregation, exercising caution in an era when disenchanted Democrat segregationists like Governor Strom Thurmond of South Carolina were running for president, rallying the support of like-minded white southern voters under the Dixiecrat banner. While his opponent, the incumbent Democrat Gordon Weaver Browning, proudly proclaimed his segregationist views, Clement remained silent on the issue. Although he exhibited no discernible racial animus, Clement never publicly questioned the Jim Crow policies codified in the Tennessee Constitution, which, since 1870, had banned the marriage of "white persons with Negroes, mullatos, or persons of mixed blood" and provided that "no school . . . allow white and Negro children to be received as scholars together in the same school."[29]

With law and order a trope of American political campaign rhetoric, it was not surprising that Browning and Clement faced off on the subject of who would protect the citizens of Tennessee better. Clement's supporters, among whom, oddly, was the more conservative of Nashville's two daily newspapers, the *Banner,* accused Browning of overseeing a virtual open door policy on pardons, accusations that arose as a result of an incident involving a pardoned rapist who soon after being released became a repeat offender.[30] Clement seized this opportunity to go on the attack. Browning, an obdurate, ill-tempered character under the best of circumstances, took the bait, proclaiming, "If it had not been for the pardoning power of God Almighty, Frank Clement would have been in Hell long ago." The irony was that, as governor, Clement "slowed the pace of pardoning, while increasing clemency through commutation." From 1949 to 1953 Browning granted 131 pardons, compared to 13 approved by Clement from 1953 to 1959.

Browning always seemed to be a step or two behind Clement, who proved himself to be a fierce, skillful campaigner. This, coupled with his exuberance and an exhausting schedule of public speaking, solidified his image in the minds of sympathetic Democrats as an indefatigable force of nature; he was youthful (Browning's age, sixty-one, was an issue), brimming with confidence, and ready to lead Tennessee into the future. As the campaign intensified, so did Clement's attacks. He accused Browning of fiscal inefficiency and, in one of his more egregious moments of grandstanding, publicly chastised him for not investigating the murder in 1951 of the Polk County dissident Democrat and political operative August Lewis. Sounding more like a preacher than a gubernatorial candidate, Clement concluded his remarks with hellfire-and-brimstone urgency, pointing at the crowd and shouting, "Murderers of August Lewis, defilers of democracy, your days are numbered!"[31]

Browning's best efforts proved to be futile. In the final tally he received 38 percent of the vote, Clement 47 percent, and the remaining 15 percent was divided between two other candidates. It was hardly a landslide, but it was a victory, and in the November general election Clement trounced his Republican opponent, R. Beecher Witt, to become, at the age of thirty-two, the nation's youngest governor.

Clement's election was bad news for Warden Swafford. During every campaign, Clement kept a list titled the "ten-point program of progress," one of which was prison reform. He often spoke of a program that "looks not only to punishment" but emphasized "rehabilitation when possible." Despite his good intentions, however, the state prison system was something "[he] never succeeded in reforming." Swafford's iron-fisted rule ended abruptly when the newly elected governor announced that thirty-three-year-old James "Droopy" Edwards, an old friend from high school, would replace Swafford. (Edwards's nickname came from an episode in high school when he was referred to by one of his teammates on the basketball team as "droopy drawers." The name stuck. Even in personal correspondence Clement often referred to Edwards as Droopy).

Edwards's credentials indicated he was the right man for the job: a Marine combat veteran who served in the Second World War, a stint with the military police, an executive officer in the Tennessee National Guard's police battalion and, most important, a firm believer in Dwight's salvation-minded Auburn paradigm, especially the concept of economic self-sufficiency. Although Swafford was surprised and somewhat bitter about his unceremonious dismissal, everything about Edwards's resume indicated he would be a younger, less demagogic version of Swafford: a no-nonsense law-and-order warden.[32]

The truth was that Edwards was the antithesis of Swafford. A progressive, reform-minded prison administrator, Edwards believed that men were sent to prison as punishment, not for punishment. His main goal as warden, in keeping with the Auburn model, was to provide inmates with work skills necessary to facilitate their return to society. As far as Edwards was concerned, this goal was simple and obvious, and its benefits, lower taxes and reduced recidivism, afforded an assured rebuttal to the criticism of those who felt the institution was coddling society's undesirables. The rehabilitative model espoused by Edwards was based on the theory that the convict's imprisonment was the result of one poor life decision. The more humane approach to prison was that after doing the time they would return "once again to contribute meaningfully to the social order." This was the dominant ideology of the 1950s based on the commitment that if respected as humans, the criminal will respond in kind.[33]

Although deemed by some too radical for the time, Edwards considered his prison reform policy simply a matter of common sense and the reputation he developed as a maverick progressive somewhat overstated. As much as he represented a near-total break with Swafford's graveyard, he believed in a stern approach to prison management. But, unlike Swafford, Edwards was a hands-on warden, a micromanager who believed in being friendly and accessible to the inmate population, yet tough and inflexible when necessary. His mettle was tested soon after he took the job: a large group of prisoners protested a decision to revoke keys to the master locks controlling a tier of cells. The keys had been given to certain trusted prisoners who functioned as inmate turnkeys under Swafford. And while the deputizing of inmates was common in prisons, the system was riddled with abuse in that nearly any inmate who wanted to could get a set of keys allowing him easy passage from cellblock to cellblock. The protesting inmates stayed in the prison's central yard and refused to return to their cells. Edwards locked all the cell entrances and told the prisoners they were welcome to stay in the yard but should plan to do so all night. As their resolve weakened from standing for hours in a cold, steady drizzle, Edwards ordered the yard flooded with searchlights. The prisoners quickly returned to their cells.[34]

"I felt that part of my purpose as warden was to get in touch with the prisoners, treat them well, and keep everything above board," Edwards remembers. "I was accessible to the inmates, but I never got too close. Maintaining the separation between warden and inmate was important."[35] From the Prisonaires' point of view, the serendipitous circumstances of Clement's election as governor and his appointing of Edwards as warden cannot be overstated. In fact, the group wrote and recorded a song about Clement that included the lyric "Let me tell 'bout the man from Tennessee / He's a God-fearing man; he's not on his own, / He gets his orders straight from the throne." Johnny recalled, "They were really interested in the rehabilitation program, they were backing us 100 percent," adding that among the most welcome policy changes was the immediate cessation of corporal punishment. "Before [Clement] got here it was slavery," Johnny remembers. "They had a big long strap . . . and they beat you, just beat you to death, man . . . the blood be runnin' like water." During one of his first trips to the penitentiary Clement asked to see the Swafford-approved "whoopin' strap." Holding it aloft, he told the assembled inmates, "This is what I think of beating human beings," and he reached into his pocket, pulled out a large knife, and cut the strap into pieces. As Johnny tells it, the inmates began "hollerin' and goin' on . . . he cut it up all the way, it might not sound like much, man, but let me tell you . . . they were beatin' people like flies . . . it was terrible."[36]

Still, Clement's elimination of the brutality perpetrated by the guards only slightly reduced the reality of prison violence. For a teenage inmate, even a badass one from north Nashville, to be part of a larger adult inmate population of hard timers and lifers was a severe test of even the most finely honed survival skills. "If the inmates didn't like you," Johnny flatly affirms, "you couldn't make it—they'd kill you."[37]

CHAPTER FOUR

Men Singing Together

Why should the world be overwise,
In counting our tears and sighs
Nay, let them only see us, while
We wear the mask

—Paul Laurence Dunbar, *We Wear the Mask*

It is impossible to imagine a time when Johnny wasn't singing, if only for fun and what little pocket change he earned working the streets of north Nashville. In prison, however, singing took on far greater meaning, becoming both a strategy for surviving the institution's routinized brutality and a way of creating a less oppressive alternative reality. Johnny was regularly beaten by guards and other inmates: "They never did beat me like they would some of them, but they used to beat me."[1] Raised in a religious household, Johnny didn't experience a full-fledged, postincarceration evangelical rebirth, but he "did a lot of praying . . . and everything I asked for it seemed like the good lord gave to me . . . I said let me organize a singing group, it may sound like kid's stuff, but it's true."[2] He was also singing more gospel, the first music he remembers singing, a rich, musical tradition that has given generations of African Americans "a secret language of solidarity, a way of articulating oppression, a means of cultural resistance, and a cry of hope."[3] Gospel's tradition of resistance through ritual and its ability to offer an outlet for individual feelings connected to the shared struggle of a disenfranchised community were probably second nature to Johnny, and to the other Prisonaires as well. Like chain-gang singing and prison work songs, gospel singing as a form of political and cultural resistance historically rises in opposition to the forces of restriction and containment, suggesting how music can function in profoundly utopian ways. George Lipsitz, writing about the gospel singer Bessie Griffin, articulates a sentiment congruent with the harsh reality of the Prisonaires. "[She] learned covert resistance from a culture that had developed it into a fine art . . . posing more direct challenges to power. Griffin's community may have paid a terrible price for their inability to confront oppression directly, but they also preserved their dignity and self-worth by asserting faith in some kind of ultimate justice."[4] For the Prisonaires, the act of singing gospel music was emancipatory, providing them with an opportunity to carve out a social living space and form a strategy for survival and collective consciousness that as inmates, musicians, and African Americans afforded them temporary solace from the brutal reality of prison.

When Johnny arrived at the penitentiary there were already a handful of gospel groups, but they were mostly disorganized and given to constant fighting and fluctuating membership. Ed Thurman and William Stewart belonged to one of the more stable lineups, and when one of the members was remanded to solitary and never returned (it was assumed he had been beaten to death), Johnny was given the opportunity to show off his clear, powerful tenor voice. Although Glenn Swafford never encouraged the singers the way Frank Clement and James Edwards did, he allowed inmates occasional opportunities to sing, such as during work details and out in the recreation yard, thereby exhibiting the harsh benevolence of a plantation owner. Johnny made the most of his circumstances by practicing whenever he could, often singing with a metal bucket over his head, a technique, he said, that made him a more nuanced singer while increasing his power and range. "I started singing in my cell with a bucket over my head for the echo, and I could hit the high notes with the bucket. Young, stupid, I didn't know what I was doing, but I was hitting them [notes]." It wasn't long before everyone knew about the singing inmate who practiced with a bucket on his head, and that drew the attention of the prison's chaplain, Pickins "Picky" Johnson. Johnson asked Johnny if he was interested in singing at prison church services, and he agreed but only if Johnson could make arrangements for the group to regularly rehearse. "Picky Johnson made it possible for us to come to the chapel and practice in one of the rooms back there," Johnny recalls. "So we was practicing day in, day out. . . . Some people say we were better than we thought we was. But we started working in these different songs and we ended up being pretty good."[5]

When Edwards assumed control of the penitentiary, one-third of its twelve hundred prisoners were under the age of twenty, and of that segment of the prison population nearly 80 percent were black. In the segregated South of the 1950s, just prior to the U.S. Supreme Court's landmark ruling in *Brown v. Board of Education,* segregation behind prison walls was also common but Edwards considered that to be incidental. There were black and white wings and segregated dining rooms and sleeping areas, but all work details, athletic teams, and common areas were integrated, as were audiences for musical performances and professional wrestling matches. Edwards's arrival meant increased opportunities for the as-yet-unnamed gospel group to practice and perform. His very first day on the job, he heard about the singing inmates and, as was his style, sought them out. He had a personal approach that greatly differentiated him from Swafford, who was, by all accounts, imperious and inflexible. Edwards was good-natured and sociable but always cognizant of reinforcing the essential, immutable hierarchy of the relationship between warden and prisoner. He chose not to sequester himself in his office, preferring to walk the yard and dining areas talking to the inmates and treating them, irrespective of their crimes, with basic decency.

The singing group kept practicing and performing at church services and prison talent shows. The shows were organized by a white inmate named Bob Brassell, who claimed to be the group's manager and, in Johnny's frank estimation, "got something like what you would call excellent." They also sang at the death house for inmates, black and white, awaiting execution. Electrocution had replaced hanging in Tennessee in 1915, and over the next forty-five years 124 inmates were put to death, nearly 70 percent of them African Americans convicted of murder, rape, and assault with intent to ravish. That Johnny, Stewart, and Thurman, the three Prisonaires convicted on such charges, were not executed is nothing short of remarkable. "I saw a lot of innocent men go down in there," Johnny recalls ruefully. "I will never forget one time a man kept saying, 'Lord God, they're killing me for nothing' . . . I never will forget that. . . . I believe[d] him [and] still believe him right today."[6] During his three years as warden Edwards supervised five executions. A lifelong supporter of capital punishment, he admits that this was, without a doubt, the hardest, most distasteful part of the job.

For Clement it was unbearable. He opposed the death penalty and enforced its use only with great reluctance. According to his biographer, Lee Seifert Greene, "Governor Clement always said that he had sent no man to death who had not in those final moments confessed his guilt to him. To a national press animated by skepticism and hatred of the fundamentalist evangelical religion that Clement followed, such conversions would appear cynical and hypocritical. But there was no publicity, no show, no votes to be garnered, nothing but unhappiness and misery, and it is not believable that the governor could have gone through these sad encounters as a publicity stunt."[7]

The group's nucleus, Johnny, Stewart, and Thurman, was solid, but other members drifted in and out. One day Johnny heard Marcel Sanders singing to himself, as was his habit during mealtime, in a rich, sonorous bass voice that didn't seem to fit a man so slightly built—at just under six feet, he weighed a mere 150 pounds. Initially hesitant to join, Sanders relented when the other members cajoled him into anchoring the group, completing a harmonically airtight quartet. The addition of Junior Drue was pure happenstance. Johnny heard him audition for the prison talent show and thought he sang like Bill Kenny of the Ink Spots, who happened to be one of his musical heroes. It was agreed that the tenor voices of Johnny, Thurman, and Drue would balance well with Stewart's baritone as long as Drue and Thurman understood that Johnny would remain the lead vocalist. Edwards, who admits to being a fan from the moment he heard them, did what he could to offer them opportunities to rehearse (usually in the laundry room or the showers) and saw their singing as a validation of his and Clement's goal of instituting a new, progressive program of penal reform that emphasized rehabilitation and skills training rather than punishment.

Yet Edwards was a pragmatist, and he understood that these inmates could not be treated, overtly anyway, in a manner that was deemed to be preferential. Even after the initial success of "Just Walkin' in the Rain"

Edwards observed, personally and anecdotally, little if any hostility by guards and other inmates toward the group owing to their celebrity status.[8] Johnny, however, remembers a more violent reality: "[Some inmates] set a trap to knock me off, they tried to electrocute me one time, they had it fixed, this room, and I'm getting ready to open the door to go iron my clothes and a guy named Curly knocked my hand out of the way. He said, 'Johnny, you're supposed to be dead.' I said, 'What are you talking about?' He picked something up and said, 'Watch this.' He threw it against the door and [he makes the sound of an explosion]. A lot of guards didn't like the idea that the niggers were going out singing . . . a lot of people wanted to kills us . . . fellow prisoners and the guards wanted to set it up, the guards set up for a lot of people to get killed in those days. They wanted Johnny bad, they wanted to kill that nigger."[9]

On June 16, 1953, six months into his tenure as warden, Edwards made his case for prison reform before the Nashville Exchange Club. Founded by a group of civic-minded businessmen in 1920, the Exchange Club rallied under the credo "Unity for Service" and pledged to pursue "the unselfish giving of service to community and nation and to those less privileged."[10] Squarely in the pre–civil rights and prefeminist tradition of the "old boys' network," the Exchange Club was exclusively white, male, and solidly upper middle class. A glance at the membership directory of 1954 shows a number of physicians, lawyers, accountants, retail executives, and even the city fire marshal. A formidable and influential group, they were among Nashville's powerful movers and shakers, and Edwards knew it was important to get their support for his and Clement's prison reform initiatives.

To that end Edwards went on the attack in his speech, decrying the Tennessee prison system as being "fifty years behind the times." Calling prison conditions deplorable, he noted that the facilities had become little more than "receiving stations" where inmates did their time and were released with "a bus ticket and a dollar-and-a-half to get to their homes."[11] He then detailed his efforts, all of which were carried out with Clement's blessing, to improve living conditions in the prison, train inmates so that they acquired work skills, increase the prison's outside contract work, and improve the quality and amount of food served to inmates. In closing, Edwards somewhat provocatively suggested that prisoners "need a job when they leave, but they also need more than that." Although he didn't specify what that "more" might be, it's clear that, as far as he was concerned, penal reform was an ongoing process that required a commitment from the outside world to continue the efforts begun in prison. Dramatically driving his point home, he concluded his speech by introducing the penitentiary's "prison quintet" in their first public performance. As described by a reporter for the *Banner*, "This group of Negro Singers which has already recorded several songs was loudly applauded by the civic club members."[12]

Showcasing the prison group in such a manner was a bold, provocative, and savvy move by the new warden. Though he admitted to having little musical knowledge and claimed no musical ability, Edwards knew intuitively that the smooth, melodic, gospel-inflected sound of the Prisonaires would go over well with the members of the Exchange Club. This group of singing negroes illustrated the range of possibilities available to inmates as well as Edwards's keen understanding of how the image of black convicts-turned-singers (especially ones that eschewed the raucous R&B or anything resembling rock and roll) would be positively received by a public comfortable with the circumscribed role of African Americans as entertainers. Edwards's intentions were undoubtedly honorable, but they also reflected a need to reaffirm the prison's rehabilitative efforts.

The conduct of the Prisonaires reveals a complex combination of accommodation and resistance: singing in prison gave them a sense of identity that restored their dignity, served as a means of cultural representation, and provided them with a strategy for survival, all of which is complicated by the fact that they were also acting as the chief representatives in the legitimation of the prison's institutional discourse—they were allowed to express themselves publicly, but only under circumstances that reinforced the prison's hierarchical organization and power. As liberal as Edwards was, he would not have allowed the group to record songs that spoke directly to their prison experience or were in any way critical of the institution. Along with serving as a powerful example of the limitless potential of penal reform, also communicated was that prison had saved these men and in so doing made the performance possible.

Edwards's best intentions notwithstanding, the Prisonaires, as de facto ambassadors for Clement's penal reform, resembled a kinder, gentler prison work gang. They may not have worn leg irons or prison garb when they performed, but even when attired in matching suits the group was shackled to an image as suffocating and confining as prison itself. As demand for their talent increased, especially after the success of "Just Walkin' in the Rain," so too did the money they earned, something that held great appeal for Edwards and his modern iteration of the Auburn system's self-sufficiency. Perhaps they were partly complicit in their own victimization—after all, being a convict-entertainer is better than simply being a convict—but the group was doubtless aware that a career and whatever temporary freedom singing afforded them was predicated upon the unique marketability of their status as convicts. Every performance by the Prisonaires included a testimonial in which one member would recount and apologize for the mistakes that had led to his incarceration (such apologies must have been galling to Johnny) as a way of reinforcing the very essence of prison rehabilitation, namely, that even the hardest criminals could be redeemed. Generally, albeit with slight variation, one member would come forward and speak directly to the audience: "We, the Prisonaires, are grateful to be a part of the rehabilitation program at the Tennessee State Prison which was set up by the warden and governor. And we hope you will say a special prayer for us in the group and for the other men here. And we hope you [receive] great joy. We want you to know we feel very happy to perform these songs for you."[13]

After the group had sung a few well-known gospel songs, Johnny would be called out front to offer a brief encomium to his fellow bandmates, the warden, and the governor before singing "Just Walkin' in the Rain": "I want to thank you fellows for the help you've given me—helping me to compose this song 'Just Walkin' in the Rain,' of course, I'm only a cowriter along with another inmate Mr. Robert Riley. We've written quite a few songs—this place is loaded with songwriters—I'm just very happy to be able to say that I thank God for making it all possible.

Most of all, I thank these fellows and our dear beloved warden and governor of the state. If it hadn't been for their help we couldn't have got the song in the free world."[14]

For Clement and Edwards it was fundamentally important that the group's stories move audiences, offering proof that, regardless of the circumstances that landed them in prison, they had turned their lives around. For the Prisonaires, short of declining all offers to perform in public, there were no other options.

CHAPTER FIVE

Music City, USA

[By the 1820s] there was not a city in the United States of equal size that showed as much interest in music as Nashville.
—F. G. Davenport, *Cultural Life in Nashville on the Eve of the Civil War*

Two decades before it became internationally known as "Music City, U.S.A.," a recording and music publishing hub built on hillbilly, gospel, and rhythm and blues music, Nashville was a radio town. In the spring of 1922, WDAA, broadcasting from the campus of Ward-Belmont finishing school, one of the South's preeminent women's academies and the alma mater of one Sarah Ophelia Colley Cannon, or, as she was more widely known, Minnie Pearl, became Nashville's first radio station. "Invisible waves really were spreading out from the school's roofs like ripples in an ethereal pond," writes the cultural historian Craig Havighurst, "racing north right through the walls of the sturdy homes on Sixteenth and Seventeenth Avenues . . . [rippling] east across Centennial Park with its mute majestic Parthenon; west across the Civil War battlements of Fort Negley; and south to Franklin, Brentwood, and dozens of surrounding burgs . . . they crackled against the bell towers of the city's mighty universities—all-white Vanderbilt and all-black Fisk." Nearly two years after the auspicious debut of WDAA, the city's airwaves were further energized by the sounds emanating from a host of new stations: WABV, WEBX, WDAD, WSIX, WBAW, WCBQ (the station was established by the First Baptist Church, and its call letters stood for "We Can't Be Quiet"), and two stations that would help define the city's rich musical history, WLAC and WSM.[1]

Launched in 1926 as a promotion and publicity outlet for the Life and Casualty Insurance Company, WLAC was initially a noncommercial station broadcasting only a few hours a day. By 1928 it had become an affiliate of the CBS radio network, increased its signal power from one thousand to five thousand watts, and soon became known as the South's Master Station. Its motto was "Health, Thrift, Entertainment, and Education." However, it wasn't until the early 1940s that WLAC became a radio force, not just in Nashville but over a remarkably large geographic expanse. By 1942 the station became one of only sixty-four in the nation to boast a fifty-thousand-watt clear channel signal—on most nights its signal reached as far west as the Rocky Mountains and as far south as Kingston, Jamaica—along with an atypically progressive attitude toward its programming that allowed disc jockeys to play virtually whatever they wanted.[2] A farsighted idea to be sure, but one born of necessity since CBS had drastically reduced its evening programming, forcing the station to use local DJs to fill the empty air. Beginning in the fall of 1945, Gene Nobles anchored the late-night show that mostly featured the music of white swing artists until a group of black students from either Fisk or Tennessee State University, some of them ex-servicemen attending school on the GI Bill, sneaked into the studio and asked Nobles if he'd consider playing some of their favorite performers.

Almost immediately, the complexion of WLAC's late-night playlist darkened considerably, as Fats Waller, Louis Armstrong, Pete Johnson, Billie Holiday, and Louis Jordan, among others, regularly aired on Nobles's show. "To the astonishment of Nobles and his employers," notes William Barlow, "the race-record experiment provoked a flood of mail (mostly from out of state) pleading for more. Within a year, WLAC was devoting its entire late-night schedule to black appeal music shows."[3] In the late 1940s two equally important DJs, Bill "Hoss" Allen and "John R" Richbourg, who some listeners erroneously assumed were black, joined Nobles, and together the trio solidified the station's reputation as an R&B powerhouse with millions of enthusiastic, devoted fans.[4]

WSM is better known and documented for being the radio station where Nashville's internationally known sobriquet, Music City, USA, was coined, and for being inextricably linked to country music for the past nine decades via the *Grand Ole Opry.* Founded by the National Life and Accident Insurance Company (a competitor of Life and Casualty Insurance Company) WSM ("We Shield Millions") went on the air on October 5, 1925, and was by all accounts a well-financed, first-class operation. Edwin W. Craig, the son of National Life's owner and president, Cornelius Craig, was convinced that radio was the perfect "new media" with which to spread the gospel of insurance, and he spared no expense in an effort to reach a growing audience of uninsured: "WSM's room was furnished like a parlor, with an ebony Steinway grand piano, wing-back chairs, frilly floor lamps, a rococo desk, and a crystal chandelier."[5] The station also boasted one of the most powerful signals in the South, which at the time was a mere one thousand watts. Seven years after its debut, WSM erected a massive radio tower just south of Nashville in Brentwood, made the jump to fifty thousand watts, and almost immediately became known as the "Air Castle of the South."[6]

More famously, WSM's contribution to Nashville's emergence as a center of country (or hillbilly, as it was known at the time) music began on the evening of November 28, 1925, when the seventy-five-year-old James Donald Thompson, widely known to his friends and kinfolk as Uncle Jimmy, entertained the listeners of the *WSM Barn Dance* by digging deep into his vast repertoire of old-time fiddle tunes. Hosted by the station manager, George D. Hay, the program was an immediate hit, and in 1927 Hay, in an oft-told moment of extemporaneous on-air inspiration, renamed the program the *Grand Ole Opry.* While the Opry provided the foundation upon which the nascent country music industry was built, another salient factor was the influx of over thirty thousand rural migrants to Nashville in the 1920s, many of them drawn to the city for jobs, education, and, especially, fun. Country music, with its tropes of family, faith, and the simplicity of rural life, offered solace to these new city dwellers and a sense of connectedness to a world they had left behind.[7]

Despite the Opry's popularity and national prominence, Nashville's transformation into Music City, USA was a post–Second World War phenomenon reflecting the city's diverse musical culture. David Cobb, the WSM announcer who coined the expression, was referring to a myriad of genres that, along with country, included bluegrass, MOR pop, gospel, and R&B. Other factors contributed to the change. Nashville's geographical centrality—twenty-four states are within a six-hundred-mile radius—made it the preferred hub of touring musicians, many of whom had to return frequently to the city to fulfill their quota of twenty-six appearances per year as members of the Grand Ole Opry. Broadcast Music Incorporated (BMI), the performing rights organization founded in 1940 by the National Association of Broadcasters to rival the monopolistic, middlebrow American Society of Composers, Authors and Publishers (ASCAP), generated a sizable amount of money through performance licensing and provided a home for many country, blues, and R&B songwriters not welcome at ASCAP. Most significantly was the city's emergence as a music publishing hub, beginning with the founding of the Acuff–Rose Publishing Company in 1942 by the Opry star Roy Acuff and the Tin Pan Alley songwriter Fred Rose. Rose, who exhibited genuine honesty and evenhandedness in his business dealings, was a welcome rarity in the industry, engendering the loyalty and respect of the songwriting community in Nashville. The success of Acuff–Rose led the way for the establishment of other publishing companies oriented toward country music in the 1940s and 1950s, including Hill and Range Songs, Cedarwood Publishing, and Tree Publishing.[8]

While country music was the engine driving the machine, it is disingenuous to suggest that Nashville's rise to musical prominence rested solely on the fortunes of that genre and its mostly white musicians. The initial enthusiastic public response to Uncle Jimmy Thompson notwithstanding, an equally compelling argument can be made that the roots of Nashville's commercial music history lie in the late nineteenth century with the Fisk Jubilee Singers, a singular moment insofar as their international popularity was a reflection of the city's importance as a center of black religious music. Thomas Talley, a chemistry professor at Fisk University and an amateur folklorist went to great lengths and considerable personal expense to document the music of African American string bands in middle Tennessee in the 1920s. Also at Fisk, the musicologist and native of Nashville John Wesley Work III, who had recorded the banjoist Nathan "Ned" Frazier and the fiddler Frank Patterson, chronicled

African American sacred and secular music in Tennessee and Mississippi, accompanied Alan Lomax to Coahoma County, Mississippi, and was present at the first recordings made by Muddy Waters, whom Work also interviewed, in 1941. Work's contributions to this important field research, which Lomax deemphasized in his musicological memoir *The Land Where the Blues Began* (1993), went unheralded and unrecognized for years.[9]

In 1949 the Tennessee State Collegians, led by the jazz trumpeter Chick Chavis and voted Best College Band by the influential African American newspaper the *Pittsburgh Courier,* took their up-tempo swing sound from the campus of Tennessee A&I all the way to Carnegie Hall. The drummer in the band, Paul Broome, told the music historian Martin Hawkins that in the thirties and forties "Nashville was loaded with black jazz. That was the music the white musicians sought out to listen to and jam with after the hotel ballrooms were closed." Although postwar urban redevelopment meant that some of the city's more infamous nightclubs were forced to close, throughout the forties and fifties white and black club-goers had a surfeit of choices featuring jazz, blues, and dance music: the Del Morocco and Club Revillot in north Nashville; the New Era Club and Doc Mandel's Roadhouse downtown; the Carousel, the Unique, and the Gaslight in Printers Alley; Brentwood had the Stork Club and the Palms; the Skyway was on Murfreesboro Road; the Wagon Wheel on Highway 100; and dozens more, all of them "magnets for visiting businessfolk and for local musicians looking to play all night."[10]

While radio, nightclubs, and a growing business infrastructure were transforming the city's musical landscape, Nashville had yet to establish itself as a record town. Aside from a commercial cylinder company and seven-inch aluminum discs pressed by the Houck Piano Company, Music City, USA had no viable, commercial record labels, at least not until Jim Bulleit, a thirty-eight-year-old radio personality turned entrepreneur, took the plunge. After a brief, unsatisfying teaching career, the Indiana-born Bulleit entered the music business in 1935 as a radio personality on WAIM ("The Voice of the Electric City") in Anderson, South Carolina. Anxious to move to a larger market, Bulleit was hired by WLAC, but the station later rescinded the offer on the grounds that he was too experienced. In an unusual, if not unprecedented, display of magnanimity, they agreed to help him find a better-paying position at a bigger station, WSM, where Bulleit hosted an early morning show "[that alternated] news, records, and live singing acts in 15 minute segments." Leaving WSM after a couple of years to try his hand at talent booking, Bulleit became convinced that a city so saturated with music, not to mention being the home of one of the most popular radio programs in America, needed a record label to tap into the potentially lucrative market. That potential was currently being exploited by the talent scout and recording director of Columbia Records, Art Satherley, who in 1944 had signed Opry performers Bill Monroe and his Blue Grass Boys, the Old Hickory Singers, and Curley Edwards and the Georgia Peach Pickers, among others. With fifteen hundred dollars of seed money supplied by the jukebox operator and record wholesaler Conrad Vertre "C.V." Hitchcock and fifteen hundred dollars of his own money Bulleit launched the Bullet Recording and Transcription Company on April 25, 1946.[11]

Bullet Recording was not, however, a venture without considerable risk. However exciting the mid-1940s were for the record business, they were also difficult. The popularity of swing music coupled with the growing ubiquity of jukeboxes aided in the recovery from the economic devastation of the Great Depression. Still, record sales were nowhere near their predepression peak of $100 million in annual revenue. Other factors were not helping matters: less than 30 percent of homes had phonographs, a shortage of shellac, the resin used in the production of 78-rpm discs, during wartime limited production, and in 1942 a strike that was to last for eighteen months was called by James Petrillo, the president of the American Federation of Musicians, thereby banning union members (defined as one who played an instrument, which meant that, according to the AFM, vocalists were not musicians) from entering a recording studio until the union and the record labels reached a royalty settlement. As a result of the strike there were no new commercial instrumental recordings until Decca and Capitol came to terms with the union in 1943 and Victor and Columbia the following year.

Last among the industry's problems, the city had a dearth of record retailers. A number of electrical appliance and furniture stores stocked records, but there was only one proper record shop, Louis Buckley's on 8th Avenue North, which opened in 1939. Fortunately for Bulleit the timing was good, as within a year of the launch of his label record stores were popping up everywhere. In 1946 the fifty-four-year-old Ernie Young, itching for a new challenge after a number of semisuccessful business ventures, jumped headfirst into the world of record retailing by opening the Record Mart (later Ernie's Record Mart) on Third Avenue just off Broadway in downtown Nashville. Less than a year later the Texas-born Opry star Ernest Tubb opened his eponymous record shop, which, in 1951, moved to its larger (and current) location on lower Broadway. Twenty-five miles northeast of Nashville in Gallatin, the electrical appliance storeowner Randy Wood noticed that while he couldn't move any of the classical and pop titles he carried, more and more customers were requesting R&B songs they heard on WLAC. Three years later, in 1950, with considerable advertising help from WLAC, Wood moved the appliances out to make room for the twenty thousand titles he now carried. The newly rechristened Randy's Record Shop, like Ernie's Record Mart, became one of the nation's largest mail-order record houses. Both Young and Wood, perhaps inspired by Bulleit, would also make the transition from mail-order retailer to independent label owner, Young with Nashboro and Excello, and Wood with Dot Records.

Bullet was modestly successful at first. Brad Brady and his Tennesseans, who were the soon-to-be-famous record producer Owen Bradley and members of his dance band, had a fluke hit with "Zeb's Mountain Boogie," which prompted Bulleit to record as many Opry performers as he could who were not already under contract, a group that included Minnie Pearl and Pee Wee King. A lifelong fan of gospel, Bulleit tapped into Nashville's rich tradition of white and black sacred singing, recording the John Daniel Quartet and the Fairfield Four. But when he decided to record Cecil Gant, whom he described as "a small black feller who never did record a thing that didn't sell and make money," his fortunes dramatically changed. Gant's tribute to his hometown, "Nashville Jumps," jump-started the city's R&B scene, and, quickly capitalizing on its success, Bulleit introduced his "sepia series," which, along with black gospel groups, included a growing roster of R&B performers like

Sherman Williams, St. Louis Jimmy, Wynonie Harris, and the Big Three Trio, featuring a very young Willie Dixon. Yet R&B records, even successful ones, sold in the tens of thousands; million-plus sellers were mostly confined to mainstream (read: white) pop music. According to Hawkins, Bulleit's desire to record pop songs was no secret: he simply couldn't afford to hire a full orchestra, a requirement on nearly every pop record.[12]

Bulleit got his pop mega-hit in 1947 with "Near You" by the Francis Craig Orchestra. Craig, a native of Dickson, Tennessee, had put in nearly three decades of roadwork with his big band and was keen to live a less peripatetic life. Cut at WSM in January and released in April, by August "Near You" was the number one selling disc in the country. Bulleit, however, did not capitalize on his success. A combination of runaway ego, bad judgment, questionable taste (one business associate bluntly claimed, "[Bulleit] recorded too much bad music"), and rapidly declining sales exhausted his cash reserves. In early 1949 Bulleit sold his interests, including all artists' contracts, master recordings, and the pressing plant, to his partner, Hitchcock. Bulleit told a reporter from *Billboard,* "[My] present plans are indefinite, but [I will] make a definite decision [about my future in the record business] soon."[13] His return to the music business would take a circuitous route, but it would lead him ultimately to play an important role as the intermediary between the Prisonaires and Sam Phillips.

CHAPTER SIX

"Just Walkin' in the Rain"

If I live to be 100
I guess I'll never clear my name
Everybody knows I've been in jail

—Merle Haggard, "Branded Man"

When [the Prisonaires] would sing "Just Walkin' in the Rain," the song that Johnny Bragg wrote . . . [it] felt like he was singing you into heaven . . . it was just so beautiful it almost made you cry.

—Anna Belle Clement

Incarceration did not keep the Prisonaires from experiencing Nashville's seismic and diverse musical transformation. As stifling as life was under Glenn Swafford, he did allow the inmates to have radios and record players, and the outside musical world also found its way inside as the penitentiary became a regular tour stop for the Grand Ole Opry stars George Morgan, Carl Smith, Cowboy Copas, Ernest Tubb, Roy Acuff, and Little Jimmy Dickens, some of them brought there by Colonel Tom Parker in the years before he met Elvis. For many of the performers there was an added bonus and ulterior motive to performing before this captive audience: the opportunity to buy songs from the inmates. Colin Escott notes that prison "was a fertile source of new songs and many Grand Ole Opry stars [bought] material from black and white inmates."[1] Johnny Bragg, who had been writing songs almost from the day he was imprisoned, claims to have sold quite a few songs to visiting country musicians. "Word got out," he recalls, "that this little old nigger in the penitentiary can write anything you ask him to write . . . he's a genius.

I was the five-dollar man. If you had five dollars, you got a hit song."[2] And while it is true that Johnny sold songs and song ideas, the most audacious of his claims, one that would necessitate a major rewriting of country music history, is his assertion that he, not Hank Williams, wrote "Your Cheatin' Heart." "I had different versions for every song and four or five different ways to sing them," Johnny says. " 'Your Cheatin' Heart' had two or three different versions. . . . Hank Williams and this older white man (here Johnny is referring to Ernest Tubb) [listened] to the song and as soon as he heard it [Williams] wanted it. I sold that song for five dollars, now it's [sold] over 200 million [copies]."[3] It was in these circumstances, nearly a year after the release of "Just Walkin' in the Rain," that another famous country singer would hear the song and make a business decision that accidentally made him the conduit by which the song would find its way from the Tennessee State Penitentiary to Johnnie Ray. The singer was Gene Autry.

Of the generation of country musicians influenced by Jimmie Rodgers, Autry was the most successful and beloved. He, like Rodgers, not only combined elements of hillbilly and blues music (especially, albeit briefly, the salacious sexual references of the blues) but also emulated the cowboy style Rodgers had embraced later in his career. Moving away from the hillbilly ethos in the 1930s was a wise career move for Autry and others. The term itself, *hillbilly,* had become a pejorative noun, one freighted with images of eccentric, impoverished, mostly illiterate hillfolk inhabiting the darker recesses of a world best described as antediluvian. The cowboy, on the other hand, offered an image of rugged individualism. "No youngster in the thirties and forties," notes Douglas Green, "ever wanted to grow up to be a hillbilly, but thousands upon thousands wanted to be cowboys, and by treating the country song with dignity and respect Autry made it part of the shining good deeds and character of the cowboy."[4]

Autry's ability to indelibly codify such an image was done through music and film. Born in Tioga, Texas, in 1907, Autry was catapulted into the consciousness of mainstream American popular culture after signing a film contract in 1934 with the Mascot Company, a subsidiary of Republic Pictures, which specialized in quickly made low-budget westerns and action serials. Over the next twenty years he starred in ninety-three films for Republic, becoming Hollywood's "Public Cowboy No. 1," the most "popular and commercially successful personality with a style that combined music, personal heroism, and Victorian morality."[5] A savvy entrepreneur, Autry maximized his income by dipping into every royalty stream imaginable, from merchandising his name and image on cap pistols to owning oil wells, establishing a realty company, starting a touring company to handle his traveling shows (which routinely sold out huge venues like Madison Square Garden), and owning a radio station, KMPC in Los Angeles. Perhaps his wisest investment, however, was in one of the music industry's few durable goods: music publishing. In 1939 he'd founded his own publishing company, Western Music, and by the mid-1940s owned two other publishing firms, Golden West Melodies and Caravan Music.[6]

By 1950 Autry's film career was winding down, and he looked toward the new medium of television, becoming, in the words of the *New York Times,* "the first motion picture star to produce and appear in films for television transmission." It was a prescient decision because in 1953 Autry made his final film, *Last of the Pony Riders,* which, along with being critically derided, proved conclusively that, at the age of forty-six and sporting a paunch and toupee, he was riding a little less tall in the saddle. Nevertheless, CBS felt that a weekly half-hour television program that combined drama with comedy (courtesy of Autry's sidekick, Pat Buttram) and singing and starred a bankable Hollywood legend wasn't much of a risk. The show ran for six years but never produced high enough Nielsen numbers to place it in the top 25 most-watched programs, and, as a western, it finished a distant third to ABC's *The Lone Ranger* and NBC's *Hopalong Cassidy.*

In addition to the grind of producing a weekly television show, Autry was still on the road, and in the spring of 1954 he came to Nashville with the producer Don Law to, in Law's words, "make records every bit as good, or better than the ones he made some years ago that were fabulous sellers." Working with Law was Joe Johnson, a twenty-six-year-old graduate of Vanderbilt Law School who idolized Autry. When he was eleven Johnson met Autry and, in a life-changing moment, shook the singing cowboy's hand at a gig in Cookeville, Tennessee. The recording sessions were productive. Autry hadn't sung with such naked emotion in years. Accompanied by Johnson and the country singer Johnny Bond, Autry performed at the Tennessee State Penitentiary, where he heard the Prisonaires sing "Just Walkin' in the Rain." At first he thought the song good enough to cover and considered adding it to the tracks he had already recorded, but, ever the businessman, he first struck a publishing deal for the song with his company Golden West Melodies. Two years later, in his capacity as head of Columbia's country division, Johnson would bring the song to the attention of Mitch Miller, who was desperately looking for that elusive hit to reanimate Johnnie Ray's stalled career. For years it was thought that Autry had cut a version of the song—it's easy to imagine him doing so since it's strongly tinged with country—but he never did. Nevertheless, "Just Walkin' in the Rain" proved lucrative for Public Cowboy No. 1, as Ray's hit version earned Autry tens of thousands of dollars in royalties.[7]

As the Prisonaires featured singer and principal songwriter, though often cowriting with Robert Riley, Johnny emerged as the group's putative leader and spokesperson, overseeing a musical evolution that incorporated country music—it's unimaginable that the pervasive influence of the Grand Ole Opry and country music wasn't part of his musical grammar—with the Tin Pan Alley songs he'd learned from his grandmother Parthenia's player piano and the sweet singing of black vocal groups of the late 1940s and early 1950s into their gospel-centered songbook. Proto-doo-wop ensembles like the Sentimentalists, Charioteers, Embers, and Johnny's all-time favorites the Ink Spots featuring Bill Kenny had a major impact on the music he composed for the Prisonaires. The formula was simple: smooth, interlocking, close harmony singing articulating quintessential pop music tropes: romantic love, loss, and longing. Aficionados of harder, grittier-sounding R&B dismissively consign such singing to a subcategory of R&B considered too commercial to be authentically representative of the best of black singing. But this manner of vocalizing offered an anodyne to R&B's preponderance of opportunistic and predatory sexual politics and, as the historian Brian Ward notes, "the skill and inventiveness with which genuine emotion could be distilled from even the most saccharine lyric by the adroit manipulation of voices separated the best vocal groups from their rivals."[8]

The greatest of Johnny Bragg's five-dollar songs was the one he kept for himself, the song that transformed the Prisonaires from convicts into celebrities. "Just Walkin' in the Rain," while not doo-wop per se, certainly anticipated the genre, one that grew from a long history of African American group harmony singing that "[constitutes] one of black music's richest traditions, an art form as deeply embedded as jazz, blues, and gospel."[9] Although the term *doo-wop* as a genre designation was first used in the African American newspaper the *Chicago Defender* in 1961 to describe the Marcels' hit song "Blue Moon," the term did not enter mainstream pop music discourse until 1969 and then was retroactively (and liberally) applied to the tradition of black close harmony R&B singing that appeared in the long-sustained wake of the Bill Kenny–led Ink Spots—whose first hit, "If I Didn't Care," was recorded in 1939—and two important vocal groups they influenced, the Ravens and the Orioles.[10] It was the Orioles, featuring the lead vocalist Earlington Carl Tilghman, aka Sonny Til, who in 1948 recorded the brilliant "It's Too Soon to Know." A huge hit with black teenagers, the song solidified the group's status as arguably the first rhythm and blues vocal group and inspired countless singers to form close harmony groups of their own.[11] "Like the frenzied rhythms of bebop and the rambling, rapid-fire exhortations of the R&B deejays," writes Nelson George, "doo-wop was a unique outgrowth of postwar black America. . . . [It] represented a form of innovative innocence . . . to this day, the sound of a doo-wop record connotes vivid and remarkably unsullied images of urban adolescence."[12] Proto-doo-wop, however, was often described as deep and mournful and featured an earnest and conservatively expressed emotionalism that could, at first blush, sound melodramatic, especially when compared to the double entendre–laden, kinetic jump blues of such R&B artists as Louis Jordan, Wynonie Harris, and Benjamin Clarence "Bull Moose" Jackson. Additionally, much early R&B vocalizing exhibited a gospel tinge, the product of groups like the Pilgrim Travelers and the Swan Silvertones, whose records sold extremely well to pop music–loving audiences and, in turn, influenced many of the era's vocalists, including Johnny, who seamlessly combined the sacred with the secular. Despite being a product of its influences, "Just Walkin' in the Rain" doesn't sound out of place compared to other R&B vocal hits of the day, for example, "Gee" by the Crows, "Golden Teardrops" by the Flamingos, and "Crying in the Chapel" by the Orioles, nor does it simply mimic genre clichés.

This manner of R&B vocalizing resulted in widespread success for many black vocal groups whose songs became fixtures on the white pop charts. This "sweet" R&B permutation featuring "an idealized vision of relations between the sexes . . . increasingly eclipsed the lusty adventurism, misogyny and fatalism at the heart of the male blues tradition . . . [enabling] a new breed of young groups to spearhead the crossover of R&B."[13] It was a time of one-hit wonders and just as many, if not more, misses. According to Ward, "During the 1950s around 15,000 [of these groups] recorded for the first, and in many cases the only, time . . . by 1954 these groups accounted for more hit records than blues singers, shouters, jazz vocalists, or instrumentalists combined . . . [leading] R&B's assault on the white charts and [helping define] the diverse phenomenon called rock and roll."[14] (Interestingly, however, nearly all doo-wop histories elide any reference to the avant-garde space jazz genius Sun Ra, who made a number of doo-wop recordings in the 1950s.) The early R&B vocal groups were part of a variegated zeitgeist of black pop music in the early 1950s, one which ran the gamut from jazz to post-swing-era jump blues to electrified delta blues to gospel music. These groups were also the beneficiaries of a go-for-broke business ethos that defined the majority of the independent record labels of the forties and fifties. The conservatism and arrogance of the major labels meant that many of the best songs of this era were recorded by smaller labels like Jubilee, located in New York City and started in 1946 by the future co-founder of Atlantic Records Herb Abramson; It's A Natural and Josie, both subsidiaries of Jubilee; Old Town, located in Harlem and founded by the record distributor Hy Weiss in 1953; Red Robin and Whirlin' Disc, launched, respectively, in 1951 and 1956 by the legendary entrepreneur Bobby Robinson, who owned Harlem's famous Bobby's Records and Tape Center and who, over the course of a long career, recorded soul, blues, R&B, and hip-hop by a variety of artists that included Gladys

Knight and the Pips, Elmore James, King Curtis, and Grandmaster Flash and the Furious Five.

Many of these labels as well as better-known and more influential independents such as Atlantic, Savoy, Modern, and Chess specialized in a particular genre or style of music. In Cincinnati the businessman Syd Nathan decided that the best way to make a fortune in the record business was to sell as many records to as many people as possible, irrespective of race and ethnicity. In 1943 he started King Records, arguably the most unheralded of the big independents. From 1945 to 1960 Nathan established a business model that influenced dozens of like-minded entrepreneurs, including Sam Phillips, and "changed not only the way American music was recorded and sold, [but] changed the music itself."[15] Although Nathan originally wanted to record exclusively hillbilly music, he quickly saw the profit in R&B and released hits by singers like Wynonie Harris and Roy Brown. Nathan and King Records reinforced popular music's mulatto nature by "seamlessly [integrating] ideas from blues, rock, country, bluegrass, and R&B," an assertion borne out by a roster of talent that included the bluegrass of the Stanley Brothers, the gospel sound of the Spirits of Memphis Quartet, the R&B of Billy Ward and the Dominoes, the rockabilly of Charlie Feathers, and the nascent soul music of James Brown, whom Nathan recorded despite hating the future Godfather of Soul's first single, "Please, Please, Please," which he called "a piece of shit."[16]

Aiding in the dissemination of black pop was black radio. In cities such as St. Louis and Jackson, Mississippi, stations aggressively promoted their growing influence in the black community. In Memphis, where African Americans made up approximately 40 percent of the population by 1950, WDIA, a radio station that in 1948 had abandoned its pop and country music format for what would become known as "negro appeal" radio, proudly claimed to reach over one million black listeners. The increasing cultural impact of WDIA and of black radio in general was featured in a *Harper's* magazine article in 1954 by Alex Haley, who argued that the importance of black radio lay in how it "helped black as well as white businesses reach potential buyers, helped blacks know where they could shop without fear of harassment, provided prestigious jobs for blacks, and provided outlets for community service announcements by civic and church groups."[17] The fundamental irony was that while black radio had jump-started the R&B era, it would be mainstream pop radio, which had been playing "acceptable" black singers like Clyde McPhatter and Sam Cooke, that would bring the genre to a larger, whiter audience.[18]

The emergence of rock and roll in the mid-1950s didn't immediately kill off the R&B vocal groups—the genre was resilient and adaptable enough to be heard on both black and white radio playlists—but by the late 1950s, especially after the emergence of teen idols like Fabian and Frankie Avalon, it was showing its age. There was a doo-wop revival in the early 1960s, partly spurred by nostalgia and the formation of "white teenaged groups that [attempted] to re-create the black sound of that early era."[19] Even so, many black acts still performing in this style were referred to as anachronistic. In the summer of 1953, however, when "Just Walkin' in the Rain" was released, the song was anything but anachronistic or obsolete, and in fact, despite its compositional formalism, reflected the crossover potential of many of the R&B vocal hits of the day.

The genesis of "Just Walkin' in the Rain" was unremarkable: Johnny and Riley were on their way to work at the prison laundry and were, literally, walking in the rain when, according to Johnny, both men started "wondering what the little girls are doing," and by the time they had finished their work detail they had worked out the song's basic structure. (This was all done by ear, as neither man could read or write music.) Crucial here, something that makes "Just Walkin' in the Rain" more than just another pop song, is that it was produced within and mediated by the prison's artificially created, mostly segregated, homosocial environment. It was, like everything about the Prisonaires career, inextricably linked to their lives as convicts, including even pressing some of their records with a prison stripe label. Barring the gimmicky "A Prisoner's Prayer," composed not by Johnny or Riley but by James Proctor, a white Tennessee Bureau of Investigation employee, the group's original compositions contain few overt references to prison.

Ray Pratt has written that music generates a rich and complex variety of what he calls "enclaves of autonomy," spaces that create an alternative psychological reality, a new little world within an old one. This analysis is enormously useful in that it encourages an examination of music's potential as an "impulse of opposition to existing conventions."[20] This assumes, however, that such complex negotiation is done within sociocultural spaces defined as free. The participants in the creation of these enclaves are connected to real social situations and organizational forms that engender and reinforce support and morale. For the Prisonaires, autonomy through music happened within an environment that denies freedom and severs connections to these social situations. Further complicating this process of resistance, empowerment, and emancipation and the creation of an alternative reality is that, ultimately, prison mediates the results and mitigates success. No matter how many records they sold, or how often they performed outside the prison, or how lauded they were as performers and representatives of prison reform, in the eyes of the general public and the Tennessee State Department of Corrections they were first and foremost convicts, three of them, nominally, for life. But because their musical abilities, encouraged by James Edwards, offered them a different status as inmates, the Prisonaires were able to construct a cultural free space within a social institution in which the ability to do so is normally restricted, constrained, and repressed.

Understanding how a song like "Just Walkin' in the Rain" functions as a cultural free space requires what the historian Lawrence Levine refers to as an internal/external analysis. While its external meaning is about a failed relationship, the song's internal meaning—that is, the meaning reflecting the lived experiences of its creators—articulates a convict's life. As much as it is a song about lost love, "Just Walkin' in the Rain" is, more tellingly, a song about confinement, regret, and the struggle for identity. When Johnny sings, "people come to windows / and they always stare at me / Shake their heads in sorrow / and say who can that fool be?" the images—windows, sorrowful stares, a sense of disconnection from the outside world—form a subtle, artfully constructed commentary that, given the Prisonaires circumstances, functions as a tightly woven metaphorical rumination on the separateness of their rigidly circumscribed lives. "Just Walkin' in the Rain" engages in an elaborate process of signifying wherein meaning is appropriated, altered, or reconstructed in relation to the dominant institution. What makes these cultural components so important is that they become the creators' own, expressive of their particular worldview and lifestyles. While this method of musical deconstruction was not unique to the Prisonaires, it is subtly manifested in "the grain of a voice . . . the manipulation of harmonies and rhythms [contributes] at least as much to [the song's] meaning as any lyric. The manner in which R&B vocal groups performed their romantic ballads had the potential to modify or subvert any literal meaning."[21] This use of pop music rooted in a gospel tradition became uniquely expressive of the Prisonaires' lifestyle and worldview as inmates, where the making and remaking of meaning and the negotiation between artist and institution were forms of expression, that is, a culturally dependent discursive practice, one in which reality is mediated through language and, by extension, language is mediated by reality.[22]

This dual commentary employs a literary process known as heteroglossia, a means of expressing authorial intent in a refracted way that creates a double-voiced discourse serving two speakers at the same time expressing two different intentions: the direct intention of the character who is speaking, and the refracted intent of the author. More important is that within this refracted discourse there are two dialogically related voices, each one cognizant of the other, a concentrated dialogue or "two voices, two world views, two languages."[23] The cultural historian W. T. Lhamon Jr. refers to this use of double meaning and dialogized voices as the "codes that some apparently innocuous pop songs and other fetishized pop objects bear with them," codes that "describe how and why disdained artists deal in doubletalk to bootleg suppressed meanings into the public sphere."[24]

However, any discussion of double meaning or the articulation of resistance in "Just Walkin' in the Rain" begs an obvious and problematic question: Would this be relevant if the group in question was not made up of convicted felons or not named the Prisonaires? If one hears Johnnie Ray's chart-topping 1956 version, the listener, no matter how attentive, would not make any association with prison or incarceration. As an artist with no direct connection to prison (although twice arrested for soliciting men for sex), Ray had no apparent vested interest in conveying a suppressed meaning of convict life into the public sphere (and seemingly neither his producer/artistic director, Mitch Miller, nor his arranger, Ray Conniff, did either); therefore, one is less likely to be reminded of or search for potential subtextual meanings and metaphorical representations of incarceration. Broadly speaking, one could argue that in Ray's version any encoded traces of incarceration are effectively wiped away—they are simply not there. However, context and interpretive strategy can overemphasize one voice while subordinating another, and in doing so dormant, encoded traces are instead not simply there but temporarily erased.

For Johnny the situation differed considerably. Twenty-seven years old at the time "Just Walkin' in the Rain" was recorded, he had spent a decade behind bars, and his songwriting reflects his growing up in two worlds: the relatively free world of childhood and the unfree world of young adulthood. Whether he employed this double commentary intentionally or unintentionally is not as important as the fact that prison provides the context against which the heteroglossia becomes readable. Incarceration was arguably more real to Johnny than freedom, and for him not to interpolate his the essence of his life as convict into his songwriting would have required extraordinary restraint and self-denial. Living inside what the sociologist Erving Goffman calls a total institution, the unfree inmate is constantly penetrated by a sanctioning interaction from above, robbing him of the ability to create an individualized means of balancing needs and objectives. This constant regimentation, a loss of self-determination, enforces a routine leading to "self-selected behavior—whether of antagonism, affection or unconcern."[25] For the Prisonaires, and Johnny especially, this self-selected behavior was singing and songwriting, their only available means of self-determination and an expression of resistive agency wherein the making of cultural meaning is an integral part of the communicative practices of those who lack power and "speak a critical language grounded in local concerns."[26]

As vernacular theorists engaged in a contested dialogue with a total institution that circumscribes their lives and defines their existence as African Americans, the Prisonaires, through music, create a counter-discourse. "When definitions imposed from above simply don't match daily social experience," writes Thomas McLaughlin, "there are two choices: either deny yourself or learn to question authorized versions. Vernacular theory can be a tactic for cultural and personal survival, a recognition and rejection of personal containment."[27] The darkness and haunting beauty of the Prisonaires' recording of "Just Walkin' in the Rain" is conspicuously absent from Ray's rendition. His version is too cluttered with the technical apparatuses of Miller's and Conniff's production, which turn it into a commodity lacking the compressed power sedimented in the Prisonaires' version. Ray's glib dismissal of the song's merits ("a piece of crap") indicates that he was unaware of the powerful sentiment buried within the lyrics (it is simply not there). His and Miller's removal of the plangent R&B and gospel elements further distances the song from an African American musical tradition that emphasizes collective memory, community survival, and the construction and maintenance of dignity.

The Prisonaires, on the other hand, explore the possibilities of the song's internal meaning (it is not simply there) by eschewing artifice for simplicity, an aesthetic decision supported by Phillips. In so doing they create a densely textured pop song that in its moments of wishful thinking, self-pity, and sentimental clichés is potentially subversive, empowering and, to quote W. E. B. Du Bois, "aware that the words that are left to us are not without interest, and, cleared of evident dross, they conceal much of real poetry and meaning beneath conventional theology and unmeaning rhapsody."[28]

A little more than a year after liquidating his record label, the Bullet Recording and Transcription Company, Jim Bulleit, true to his word, made his decision, and it was to return to the music business. He wisely chose promotion and talent booking over label ownership, and, in early 1951, he was employed at KWKH in Shreveport, Louisiana, managing and booking talent for the *Louisiana Hayride,* a popular radio show regarded as a steppingstone to the more prestigious *Grand Ole Opry.* Later that year he was handling publicity for the Hadacol Caravan, "a traveling variety show of epic proportions . . . [featuring] an array of popular and country talent that included Bob Hope, Milton Berle and Hank Williams."[29] But the allure of running a record label proved irresistible, and by early 1952 Bulleit had started Red Robin Records, quickly changing its name to J-B upon learning that there was already a Red Robin label in New York. More important, the year he launched his entrepreneurial comeback Bulleit entered into a business relationship with Phillips. It was a minority partnership in which Bulleit would arrange distribution for Sun releases and occasionally act as an A&R rep. Despite being dogged by a reputation for recording too much bad music, Bulleit knew he was on to something when his friend and colleague Wilburn Clyde "Red" Wortham told him about a group of singing convicts he'd recorded at the state penitentiary.

When it came to the music business, Wortham's fingerprints were everywhere: guitar prodigy, radio show host, touring musician, songwriter, song-plugger, music publisher, studio owner, a quintessential jack of all trades. Unlike many others of equal ambition but limited ability, however, Wortham mastered and excelled in virtually every aspect of the music industry, and when his career as a musician was truncated by muscular dystrophy he turned to writing songs full time, renting office space from Bulleit.[30] Wortham had heard about the Prisonaires from Joe Calloway, a reporter at radio station WSIX. In the winter of 1953 Calloway was at the prison recording a news story on the changes being implemented by the new warden. Edwards, seizing the opportunity to publicly demonstrate his and Governor Clement's efforts at prison reform, made sure Calloway heard the Prisonaires. After listening to two songs, the impressed reporter went Edwards one better, suggesting that the group be let out to record at WSIX. It would not be the first time the group had performed outside the prison. Edwards had been semi-secretly taking the group to his home—often they were driven there by his wife, Evelyn, also known as Red—and to the governor's mansion to entertain influential guests who might help garner support for their reform efforts. The media-savvy Edwards didn't have to mull over Calloway's offer for long. He informed the group about the reporter's offer the next day, and a few days later the Prisonaires, dressed in brand-new matching, prison-tailored suits, were driven by armed guards to WSIX.

The session yielded four songs: "Baby Please," "Dreaming of You," a version of Louis Jordan's "That Chick's Too Young to Fry," and "Just

Walkin' in the Rain." The performance led to a regular spot on WSIX and the fledgling station WSOK. Founded by the white businessman Cal Young in 1951, WSOK was, insofar as there were black shareholders in the ownership group, the first black-owned negro appeal radio station in Nashville. With all-black on-air talent such as Lee "Blabbermouth" Dorms and "Bouncin'" Billy Powell and a hip, black public relations man by the name of George White, WSOK specialized in R&B and gospel, too often fighting a losing battle for listeners with the more powerful and financially solvent WLAC. Notwithstanding WSIX's and WSOK's relatively small aggregate market share, the Prisonaires, months before their first recording session at Sun and their performance before the Nashville Exchange Club, were a success, both as performers and representatives of the possibilities available to inmates under the prison's and the state's new leadership.

Red Wortham, on the other hand, was more keenly interested in making money, and, to that end, he copyrighted "Just Walkin' in the Rain," rightly hearing it as the most impressive and potentially lucrative song of the four recorded. In order to drum up interest for the song and the group, the cagey and opportunistic Wortham employed the tried-and-true music business tactic of manipulating two parties into a bidding war. He pitched the song to his old friend Bulleit, but not before first approaching Paul Cohen at Decca. In the end Bulleit got the song and the group, not because of his friendship or previous business dealings with Wortham, but because Cohen took too long to make a decision and because Bulleit sweetened the offer by pitching the Prisonaires to Phillips along with a handful of lesser artists who were, in one manner or another, tied to Wortham.

Phillips agreed to the package deal but was most keenly interested in the Prisonaires. He may have been enamored of the group's sound, but this seems an odd pairing if only because Phillips, who did admit to a fondness for the silky harmony singing of the Mills Brothers, generally preferred rougher, bluesier singers—he famously said of Howlin' Wolf's explosive voice, "This is where the soul of man never dies"—and nothing he had previously recorded, for example, Wolf, Rufus Thomas, Roscoe Gordon, Ike Turner's Kings of Rhythm, sounded like the

Prisonaires. Perhaps it was their sound coupled with a unique marketing opportunity; certainly the "singing convicts" angle would shift records. Phillips, who considered himself a politically and socially progressive, modern southerner, was also motivated by the era of change ushered in by the state's new young governor. The important next step was getting the group to Memphis. Although Phillips and Wortham both take credit, it was Bulleit who brokered the deal, convincing an initially skeptical Edwards (Memphis was, after all, quite a distance from Nashville) and an enthusiastic Clement that this one recording session would be just the thing to make the rest of the state, if not the nation, aware of their prison reform initiative. The decision, however, was not without huge risk for all involved. Had one of the Prisonaires escaped or been involved in a crime, Clement's and Edwards's reform efforts would have been ruined, jeered mercilessly by waves of negative reporting from the *Tennessean*. Phillips would have survived, but he did not want to be culpable in destroying the reputation of a governor he believed to be the greatest in Tennessee history.

On June 1, 1953, the deal was done, the daylong trip paid for not by Tennessee taxpayers but by Phillips himself: "I told the warden that we were going to pay for the guards necessary. [T]wo cars brought them over here [and] two guards came with them . . . it was really good that they came over here and did it because we were able . . . to relax them more than we would have in the maximum security prison. I think it was a real blessing that we were able to get them over to Memphis and Sun Studios." (Sun was the record label, the recording studio part of Phillips's micro-empire was known as the Memphis Recording Service) Relaxed though the group may have been, to make sure escape was not an option, the Prisonaires arrived wearing ankle shackles. Had they wanted to run, Phillips recalled, "I believe they wouldn't have gotten very far."[31]

The recording session in Memphis begs a couple of salient questions regarding the group's name. When exactly did they become the Prisonaires? And who came up with the name? Unsurprisingly, there are two conflicting stories and no clear answer. One version has it that Johnny, in a burst of creative spontaneity, came up with a name that simultaneously foregrounded their inmate status and paid homage to other gospel-based close harmony groups they admired, like the Jordanaires; that and it sounded classier than the obvious the Prisoners. This version of events alleges that they were using the name for a year or so before Edwards's arrival and, more important, that, regardless of who came up with it, it originated from within the group. The other account attributes the naming of the group to none other than Red Wortham during the group's first visit to WSIX. Either story is plausible, although the name does have panache and an obviousness one might expect from an A&R wheeler-dealer with an ear for exploitation and marketability. Calling them anything else would have been counterintuitive, at least from a business perspective, insofar as *the Prisonaires* is metaphorically imbued with the tragic consequences that landed them in the penitentiary and suggests an ultimately sadder, unironic story, something that would not have been the case had they been named, say, the Johnny Bragg Quintet. Lending credence to Wortham's assertion is that the group's name wasn't used in media accounts until after "Just Walkin' in the Rain" was released. An article in the *Tennessean* dated July 9, 1953, the day after the record was released, identifies the group as the Prisonaires. It is unknown if Edwards introduced them by that name almost a month earlier at the Exchange Club appearance, but since press accounts referred to them as the "prison quintet" and a group of "negro singers" it is likely they were not yet officially known as the Prisonaires.

The session at Sun was scheduled for 10 a.m., which meant that by the time the group arrived they had been on the road since dawn. Today, the trip from Nashville to Memphis takes nearly four hours, but the Prisonaires' journey was considerably longer given that almost all of it was made on two-lane secondary roads. Once the group arrived at the studio, Phillips, as was his style, made sure the vibe was relaxed; he wanted to rid the room of tension and any potential for performance anxiety. He suggested that the guards head next door to Taylor's Restaurant, assuring them he would be fine alone with the group. As Phillips, recalled, "I wanted to make sure that the audition wasn't [tough]. . . . imagine [black] prisoners back in those days coming to audition for a white man, and really not knowing me, that had to be a real tough call for them."[32] The stoic William Stewart, whose guitar playing and harmony singing Phillips believed was as important as Johnny's vocals in making the Prisonaires' sound, immediately impressed Phillips, as did Marcel Sanders's ability to effortlessly switch vocal parts. And Ed Thurman, despite not having the sweetest voice, had what Phillips regarded as "the most natural sounding [voice] . . . [Ed] had great command of his voice."[33]

While Phillips might have not have been thoroughly captivated by the Prisonaires' semi-jazz, proto-doo-wop sound, it is unlikely the group could have found a more understanding, more sympathetic producer. He was the perfect choice because he intuitively understood that rushing a performer new to recording rarely produced anything worthwhile. "From the beginning," he remembered years later,

> I was very much interested in exploring some paths that had not been trodden and looking for the hidden possibilities. I knew these people had not been "overly-exposed" because most of them had never had an opportunity to even be in a studio and so what I tried to do with each artist was to find his natural honesty in terms of what he liked to do regardless of what category of music it might fall into. I did not want him doing something to please somebody behind the control room glass. It was about trying to develop confidence, knowing that any audition was extremely difficult even for professionals—let alone for people who had never been tried or proven.[34]

Perhaps the first producer of the rock and roll era to have an innate understanding of the psychology of recording, Phillips believed, unwaveringly and for his entire life, that the two most important ingredients differentiating a good record from a great one were simplicity and naturalness. What he asked of the Prisonaires was straightforward and uncomplicated and represented a recording philosophy that, in tandem with the artists he recorded, effectively redefined the postwar popular music landscape: Do it to the best of your ability, and we'll go from there.

After numerous takes, the session bogged down in the late afternoon. Phillips and the Prisonaires were not terribly pleased with the results, something that Johnny blamed on his poor diction, a speech impediment Phillips called it—*just* came out as *jist, walking* sounded more like *working* and *torturing* like *torterin'*. It wasn't hopeless yet, but Phillips decided a break was in order and sent out for dinner. Then, as Johnny remembers it, help arrived courtesy of a young, presumably talented but unrecorded singer who sneaked into the studio: "Elvis [slipped] into the studio and Sam Phillips got mad. I was having trouble pronouncing the words, I could hit the notes but my diction was bad. And this little ol' guy comes out of nowhere—raggedy blue jeans, dust all over his face, 'I can help you with them words'—Sam Phillips pitched a ball, 'Boy, I've told you to stay out of here . . . we got all these nigger convicts down here [and] something'll happen if they call us down.' One thing led to another and I said, 'Mr. Phillips, give him a chance,' and that's how Elvis got his break."[35]

Like the serendipitous meetings with Billie Holiday and Hank Williams, the alleged intercession of Elvis and his salvaging of the stalled session are likely another instance of Johnny's imaginative truth. In his scrupulously researched biography of Elvis, *Last Train to Memphis,* Peter Guralnick, on the basis of interviews with Marion Keisker, a local radio personality and office manager at Sun Records and the first person to have any direct contact with Elvis, notes that the soon-to-be King of Rock and Roll did not walk through the front doors of Sun until July 18, 1953. This makes sense given that if "Just Walkin' in the Rain" did pique Elvis's interest in Sun Records, his first appearance at 706 Union Avenue came ten days after its release. Elvis was also interested in the Memphis Recording Service because of its slogan, "We Record Anything, Anywhere, Anytime," which meant he could spend four dollars to cut an acetate of the song "My Happiness" as a gift for his mother. In his book *Good Rockin' Tonight,* Colin Escott repeats Johnny's story but does so with implied skepticism, noting that Clark Porteous, a reporter for the *Memphis Commercial Appeal* who was covering the session as a human interest piece, never mentions the skinny white boy with the dusty face in raggedy blue jeans.[36] Phillips's memory of the event also casts doubt on Johnny's recollection, although his attempt at being diplomatic sounds slightly elusive and contradictory: "Johnny may very well remember Elvis coming in, I do not recall that, but I would not say that Johnny is wrong about that, I'm just saying that is a type of thing that could have happened and maybe got past me but usually that didn't happen in 706 Union because that little studio was so small it was real difficult for a mouse to go across that floor and we didn't know about it."[37] Equally hard to imagine is that the progressive Phillips would casually have used the epithet *nigger*. Johnny, who considered Phillips a decent, honorable man, chalked it up to the zeitgeist, a dehumanizing expression that had become so common in white southern discourse that it was repeated with cruel indifference. Keisker, however, went on record as stating that Phillips would never have uttered such a word and that not once in her time at Sun did she hear him do so.

Sensing that the track needed a little more instrumental heft, Phillips sent out a call for Joe Hill Louis. An adept multi-instrumentalist and Memphis legend, Louis was born Leslie Hill, the appellation Joe Louis being a reference to his formidable pugilistic skills. Also familiarly known as the Be-Bop Boy and the Pepticon Boy (Pepticon being a popular health tonic, its advertising jingle written by none other than B. B. King), Louis hosted a fifteen-minute program on WDIA, the nation's first radio station programmed by African Americans for African Americans, and had some minor success with "Gotta Let You Go," a proto–gangsta rap side he had cut in 1950. Louis's electric guitar fills were simply too rough and intrusive to be of any use on "Just Walkin' in the Rain," and once that idea was quickly abandoned, his contribution to the session was limited to Robert Riley's "Baby Please," an Ink Spots / Mills Brothers homage featuring a bluesy, bel canto lead vocal by John Drue. Years later Phillips remarked that only Stewart's guitar playing was on the finished track, which is undoubtedly true, although Louis is credited with playing on the track there is no audible electric guitar. At 8:30 p.m. the session wrapped. Phillips argued persuasively that "Baby Please" was the hit and should be the A-side; the group demurred, believing almost from the first day they sang it that there was something special, albeit ineffable, about "Just Walkin' in the Rain." Phillips remained unmoved, and on July 8, 1953, Sun 186, "Baby Please" / "Just Walkin' in the Rain" was released.

In the six weeks prior to the release of the record the group was busy. Along with their memorable appearance before the Nashville Exchange Club, Edwards was fielding a steadily increasing number of requests for the group to sing at schools, churches, and events of civic organizations.

Not long after their first appearance on WSIX, Clement asked the Prisonaires to sing at the governor's residence in what would become almost a weekly gig, always with an armed guard and occasionally driven to and from the prison by Edwards's wife, Red. Built in 1929, the governor's mansion was originally the home of William Ridley Wills, the founder of the National Life and Accident Insurance Company. The state purchased the home, which Wills had christened Far Hills, after his death in 1949. Although the residence offered all the warmth and charm of an oversized English baronial manor, Clement's frequent social gatherings were held in the mansion's somewhat more intimate upstairs, which included a small sitting room accommodating slightly more than a dozen people. At these functions Clement stressed informality, according to his sister Anna Belle, who said, "He liked for everybody to feel at home and not have to be real proper."[38] Everybody, that is, except the Prisonaires, who were expected, if not actually instructed, to act far more decorously than the invited guests.

The rules the Prisonaires had to follow were simple: know your place, speak only when spoken to, always be pleasant and polite, and, most important, stay together and don't wander off. There was never any trouble at these gatherings, never an incident because, to a man, the group knew that any attempt at escape was virtually impossible and would immediately and forever end these occasional furloughs. "They appreciated the fact they could have any kind of freedom," remembers Anna Belle Clement, "because they knew they had done wrong . . . and I think they welcomed the idea they could have a breath of air and sing and do something with their talent."[39] According to Phillips, it was at one of these gubernatorial gatherings that the Prisonaires, à la Lead Belly, very nearly sang their way out of prison by entertaining President Harry Truman with a set of gospel numbers that included "The Old Rugged Cross" and Governor Clement's favorite hymn, "Lead Me On." After an impromptu rendition of "The Missouri Waltz," the normally pugnacious Truman, allegedly overcome with emotion, told Clement that he should "pardon every damn one of those boys, anybody that's learned to do what they have in prison, and to sound like they do [has] no business behind bars."[40] Clement agreed with his assessment but doubted that his political enemies, not to mention the *Banner* and the *Tennessean,* would agree.

In November 1953 no less a periodical than *Ebony* made mention of the Prisonaires: "Self-trained for a dozen years in the bleak cell blocks of [the] Tennessee State Prison, five Negro convicts who call themselves the Prisonaires have sky-rocketed to nation-wide fame with a Sun label recording of 'Just Walking in the Rain,' a sentimental ballad written by another convict which has sold 225,000 copies." It is unknown where the *Ebony* reporter got his information, but 225,000 copies was a generous estimate. Although Phillips had declared "Baby Please" the surefire hit, disc jockeys at WSOK and every other radio station in Tennessee that picked up on the record were playing "Just Walkin' in the Rain" far more frequently. Less than two weeks after its release twenty thousand orders had poured in, requiring the efforts of record-pressing plants outside Nashville to keep up with the demand. The day after the release the group was allowed out to perform at a stock car race as the opening act for the hillbilly headliner Big Jeff and the Radio Playboys, an event MC'd by the legendary WLAC jockey and Prisonaires fan Bill "Hoss" Allen. The *Tennessean* for July 17 ran a brief story (without a byline) on the group, erroneously giving songwriting credit solely to Riley and quoting Bulleit, who noted that the record's initial sales pace was greater than that of his biggest hit, Francis Craig's "Near You." "Unfortunately for the Prisonaires," the article went on to note, "they won't be able to get their hands on any money earned from [*sic*] them by the record. It will go into the prison bank for them. However, twenty percent of it, at their suggestion, will go into the inmates fund to help fellow convicts."[41] The reality of the group's incarceration notwithstanding, the attendant publicity the song was generating was a public relations coup for Clement, confirmation that he had done the right thing by firing Swafford in favor of the reform-minded Edwards, and his public pronouncements enthusiastically reflected this: "The Prisonaires represent the hopes of tomorrow rather than the mistakes of yesterday," Clement gushed to a reporter from the *Memphis Press-Scimitar.* "If just one person is led to a better way of life thru [*sic*] their music our efforts have not been in vain."[42] In mid-August the record was favorably reviewed in the nation's two largest music trade publications, *Billboard* and *Cashbox*, making *Cashbox*'s national R&B Top 10 alongside records by B. B. King, The "5" Royales, Chuck Willis, and the Orioles.

As sales increased the Prisonaires were traveling farther from Nashville as Edwards was deluged with requests from across the state. His booking policy was decidedly informal, nothing was written down, and often Deputy Warden John Watt would arrange the performances and the group's travel—now in a sleek, new black sedan rather than a white prison van. The fee for a performance was a modest fifty dollars (or less depending on an organization's ability to pay), with 20 percent of the earnings, including record sales, going into an inmate fund. "Their unique success as recording artists," enthused the writer from *Ebony*, "is equaled, however, by their unusual custom of walking boldly out of the prison gates for church, school, and recording engagements."[43] Sometimes a successful performance would result in a donation to the Inmate Recreation and Athletic fund, as happened after a show in Cookeville at Tennessee Tech University. "We congratulate you and your staff," wrote the university representative Maurice Haste to Edwards, "along with Governor Clement and his advisors, for developing such a worthwhile rehabilitation program in the state institutions."[44] At other times a performance by the group was part of a larger fundraising effort, like the engagement at Central High School in tiny Gainesboro, Tennessee, an hour east of Nashville, which raised money for new school band uniforms.

But of all the performances during the summer of "Just Walkin' in the Rain" the most moving took place in Stewart's hometown of Hartsville. It had been thirteen years since he had left the family farm to serve a life sentence as an accomplice in the beating death of Robert Lauderdale. As reported in *Ebony*, prior to the show, Stewart was allowed to visit with his family for the first time since his incarceration, and the Prisonaires performed for nearly an hour. Although "Just Walkin' in the Rain" was what most everyone had come to hear, it was the evening's aptly chosen concluding number, the spiritual "Coming Home," that stopped the show. Sobbing audience members rushed the stage, singing in unison with the group. Ultimately, it was too much for the emotionally overwrought Stewart, who had to be led from the stage. "By the time the Prisonaires finished," affirmed *Ebony,* "there wasn't a dry eye in the house."[45]

For all the positive press generated by the Prisonaires that summer, the reform efforts of Clement and Edwards remained under constant scrutiny. There was an ongoing controversy regarding the screening of sponsors for prison parolees. Some of them were working in conditions, as described by Charles Crow, the executive secretary of the state pardons and parole board, of slave labor; some of the paroled prisoners were asking to be returned to the penitentiary. There was also the case of the thirty-five-year-old convicted murderer John Henry Watson, who had arrived at the penitentiary five months before Johnny. Watson, who worked as the stage manager for the prison variety show, had been reprimanded for drinking and was sent to the "red line" cell block, where, drunk and despondent, he hanged himself with a wire bedspring. He left behind a note that read, "I am taking my own life because no one cares for me and everybody tries to harm me. My life is miserable. It just has to be like this. I am real sorry."[46] The anti-Clement *Tennessean* saw this as more evidence that, despite the Prisonaires' success, such a controversial attempt at reform had yet to produce any meaningful change.

The *Tennessean* was certainly not alone in expressing concern for the precedent Clement was setting with the Prisonaires. After the show at Central High School, the editor of the *Jackson County Sentinel,* Fred Tardy, blasted the governor for exposing impressionable children to such hardened criminals and for creating an atmosphere that put the community at risk. With the *Ebony* article shining a national spotlight on the group and the unusual circumstances surrounding their "career" as convict-entertainers, other prison wardens felt compelled to weigh in, most notably Wilfred L. Denno, the warden of one of America's most notorious maximum-security facilities, Sing Sing prison in New York. It was his considered opinion, one reflecting a decidedly more conservative approach to penology, that such efforts were naive and misguided. Although the group was earning money that would benefit the entire prison population, Denno argued that an artificially created hierarchy, especially one that offered such benefits to a limited number of participants, would foster a pecking order that granted special privileges to a small number of inmates and would lead to internal divisiveness and violence. In order for any prison to run efficiently and quell unrest that might lead to an inmate uprising, all inmates needed to be treated the same, regardless of their talent as entertainers.

Despite the criticism and controversy, sales of "Just Walkin' in the Rain" remained brisk throughout the summer. The record was a Top 5 success in Nashville and Memphis and was making national noise on *Billboard*'s and *Cashbox*'s R&B sales charts. Thanks to the press exposure in both *Ebony* and *Jet*, the group was receiving fan mail from across the country. "The [Prisonaires] are getting from 10–25 letters a day," enthused Phillips's younger brother Jud who had recently joined the marketing and promotion department at Sun Records. "They make me think of a bunch of baby birds. They are fine boys all of them. I get great joy out of helping people like that."[47] However, anyone familiar with the fickle nature of the music business and the rapidity with which hit records—and careers—appear and disappear knew that, in order to maintain momentum, more sides needed to be cut, and soon.

The now-celebrated Prisonaires returned to Sun Studios on August 3 and recorded four songs: "Softly and Tenderly," "A Prisoner's Prayer," "My God Is Real," and "No More Tears." All agreed it was a productive session. Ike Turner, whose Kings of Rhythm had recorded "Rocket 88" at Sun in 1951 (released by Chess Records under the name Jackie Brenston and His Delta Cats—Brenston was Turner's vocalist/tenor sax player), contributed piano, guitar, and bass. Both "Softly and Tenderly" and "My God Is Real" were public domain gospel standards that Johnny had been singing since he was a child on the streets of north Nashville. "Softly and Tenderly" was cut with near palpable exuberance, Turner punching out a piano boogie intro very similar to his own "Rocket 88" and Sanders delivering a commanding, full-throated lead vocal. Johnny shines on "My God Is Real" (after all, he'd sung it countless times), but the performance Phillips captures sounds a little perfunctory, too reserved and lacking energy. The secular pop of "No More Tears," written and sung by Johnny, is structurally reminiscent of "Just Walkin' in the

Rain," right down to Stewart's acoustic guitar opening. Johnny's vocal is dynamic, and, while the lyrics are not as emotionally complex as those of "Just Walkin' in the Rain," his delivery reinforces his isolation and disconnection from the outside world ("No one knows I sit and cry / No one cares that I am blue"), a world that rarely, if ever, gives a second thought to those locked away. What distinguishes these songs—as well as nearly every Prisonaires' song written by Johnny, with or without Riley's help—from the final track recorded at this session is that "A Prisoner's Prayer," written by James Proctor, traffics in the most shameless and manipulative kind of bathos. Johnny does his best to wring some emotional depth from such lyrics as, "Dear God, please look around / and see if somewhere you can find / a place for me when I die," but he utters the words "Dear God" with such exaggerated vibrato, as if he's breaking down, that the result is more disingenuous than dramatic. Proctor's lyrics eschew symbolic expression for willful obviousness that, given the song's compositional orthodoxy, is resolutely banal.

The Prisonaires and Phillips had gotten lucky with their first record when disc jockeys and the public decided that "Just Walkin' in the Rain," not "Baby Please," was the hit. Lightning, however, would not strike twice, as Phillips chose the two gospel tracks, "My God Is Real" and "Softly and Tenderly," as the follow-up record instead of the more mainstream proto-doo-wop of "No More Tears" and the hokey, yet eminently marketable "A Prisoner's Prayer." Released in mid-September, the record garnered positive reviews in *Billboard* but was relegated to the magazine's spiritual section and struggled to find a place on the R&B charts. Not helping matters was the fact that in October, four months after its release, "Just Walkin' in the Rain" was still selling, a weekly fixture on both *Billboard*'s and *Cashbox*'s R&B Top 10. Whatever Phillips's reasoning, this decision backfired badly by not capitalizing on the momentum that had been built up during the summer. Needing to quickly put the gospel fiasco behind him, Phillips brought the group back to Memphis on October 17 to record "I Know," a song originally recorded in 1945 by the Jubalaires (a gospel version of the Ink Spots), and rerecord "No More Tears." The session yielded another finished track written by Johnny, "If I Were King," which, despite an energetic lead vocal is, at a mere 1:38, lightweight and forgettable, which may explain why it was never released. Johnny's velvety croon on "I Know" convincingly approximates the timbre of the great Sonny Til of the Orioles, and although the song does give Johnny plenty of room to show off his range and elegant phrasing, it sounds dated—a bland, safe choice. The second version of "No More Tears" has a few minor changes from the first, principal among them a more prominent role for Stewart's guitar; but the major difference was that Phillips encouraged Johnny to use his falsetto, which he does to great effect nearly two minutes into the song when he repeats the bridge. It is a striking moment, at once playful and intense, a sudden jolt that elevates the song from mundane to sublime. Although "No More Tears" was clearly the most arresting track, there was still something about it that felt unfinished. Phillips decided it would be wiser to combine the more conventional "I Know" with the bathetic "A Prisoner's Prayer." Released on November first, the record flopped.

There was, however, a more pressing issue at hand: John Drue and Marcel Sanders were up for parole. Drue, convicted of grand larceny, and Sanders, of involuntary manslaughter, were short-timers and, at the time of the October session at Sun, had already met with the parole board. Drue's release date was scheduled for October 3, and the group, with Warden Edwards's help, agreed to keep him abreast of recording sessions and public appearances so he could continue as a Prisonaire. The plan turned out to be unnecessary as, inexplicably, Drue's petition for parole was denied. It is impossible to grasp the parole board's logic. Drue was not a violent offender, and while he did have issues with alcohol that contributed to his incarceration he had been both a model prisoner and Prisonaire, trustworthy enough to become Edwards's chauffeur. Perhaps the parole board gave too much weight to his initial assessment interview in 1951, which dismissed him as a lost cause, a man who would almost certainly return to crime if given the opportunity.

Sanders's meeting with the parole board occurred nearly a month before the second session at Sun. Like virtually everything surrounding the group, the prospect of his release was newsworthy: "Prisonaire Before Parole Board Wednesday," shouted the headline in the *Banner.* Interviewed for the story, Sanders noted that he "would like to continue in the music business but [doesn't] know exactly where to start."[48] Perhaps it was that gnawing uncertainty that led him to do what in the minds of every other inmate was unthinkable—turn down his parole. This unprecedented move, combined with Drue's continued incarceration, kept the group together but was hardly the happy ending Clement and Edwards hoped for, since the whole point of their rehabilitative efforts required that convicts achieve a successful reintegration into society.

After the widespread apathy that greeted "I Know" and "A Prisoner's Prayer," no more recording sessions were scheduled. The hope was that the continued success of "Just Walkin' in the Rain" might be enough to carry them into the new year, but that required the single to maintain its current sales pace for close to seven months, a rarity for a record that was a regional hit. Despite struggling to repeat the success of "Just Walkin' in the Rain," the Prisonaires found that requests for public appearances by the group increased: they were in demand for county fairs, halftimes at football games, American Legion halls. Edwards said yes as often as he could, for it meant more positive PR and more money for the prison's recreation fund. Not once was there trouble, not once did any member of the group try to escape, even when the ideal opportunity to do so occurred on Christmas Eve 1953.

On their way to a gig at a north Nashville church, the Prisonaires' sedan sideswiped a car driven by a Nashville firefighter named James Baird. There was minimal damage to both cars, but the guard traveling with the group, along with Baird, went to a nearby house to call the police and inform Edwards of the accident. For ten minutes the Prisonaires were alone, with no shackles, not in prison garb, and in a part of town not far from where Johnny had grown up. One can only assume that there was a brief conversation among them about their situation and the possibility of simply running off, but in the end they chose to stay put. They must have reached that decision after carefully considering certain situational realities: How far could they have gone in ten minutes? Why jeopardize their career? Strictly speaking they weren't free, but being a convict-entertainer with circumscribed benefits was better than simply being an escaped convict who, when recaptured, would never again be allowed this opportunity again. So they sat in the cold until two Nashville police officers arrived. Two days later the *Tennessean*'s front-page headline "Prison Singers Left Unguarded" seemed designed to incite fear and concern, but anyone reading the story concluded it was a non-event: "[Police officer] Williams said last night that he himself did not talk to Edwards, but said his partner did. The officer said the accident was so minor, damage to each vehicle amounted to nothing more than scratches on the bumper of the Prisonaires car, and a scratch on the bumper of Baird's car. Warden Edwards said, referring to the damage to Baird's car, 'I'll get it fixed and it will only cost about a dollar.'"[49]

The trumped-up controversy surrounding the nonescape behind them, Phillips arranged another recording session. On February 2, 1954, the group returned to Sun and cut three tracks: a song written by Riley called "Don't Say Tomorrow," another homage in the style of the Ink Spots entitled "I Wish," and a third try at getting a suitable rendition of "No More Tears." Listening to these tracks, one is left feeling that both Phillips and the group were becoming increasingly frustrated and anxious over not being able to duplicate the magic of "Just Walkin' in the Rain." They also seem unwilling to risk changing or updating their sound. The instrumentation is still sparse, nothing more than Stewart's acoustic guitar, the vocal harmonies still airtight, but the songs, delivered in a soothing midtempo croon, show their age, especially when compared to the raucous R&B songs of the era. The most modern-sounding track, "Don't Say Tomorrow," is palpably exuberant, emulating the fervent, hard gospel jubilee singing of the Dixie Hummingbirds. But "I Wish," though beautifully sung, sounds superannuated, more than a decade old, and "No More Tears" is identical to the version recorded the previous October. After careful consideration and not hearing a potential hit, Phillips shelved the tracks. Exacerbating the situation was that, back in Nashville, Clement and Edwards were embroiled in a controversy that jeopardized their rehabilitative efforts as well as the Prisonaires' chances of ever again performing outside the penitentiary.

Milton Hix entered the Tennessee State Penitentiary on March 13, 1953, four months before Edwards's impassioned speech and the Prisonaires' equally impassioned performance before the Nashville Exchange Club. Convicted of killing J. H. Ammons in Chattanooga, Hix, a forty-three-year-old used car dealer, shot Ammons five times in the back after Ammons threatened to kill him for having an affair with his wife. Hix pleaded guilty to second degree murder and received a ten-year sentence. While inside he worked as a trusty, a form of prison organization nearly as old as the penal system itself in which unarmed inmates, positioned at the top of the inside world hierarchy, assisted prison employees in a number of custodial and administrative capacities. Hix was teamed with fellow trusty Eugene Helton, who was serving a ninety-nine-year sentence for murdering his girlfriend Mary Joy Delaney.

In their capacity as trusties, Hix and Helton worked at the prison's pumping station and reservoir, sharing what one newspaper report charmingly described as a four-room "comfortable little cottage" on a hillside overlooking the main prison.[50] The only barrier between the house and the outside world (even though the house was on prison grounds) was a two-foot-high stone wall. And while neither prisoner had ever attempted escape—there was little reason to, as guards left them alone, checking on them only infrequently, nothing prevented them from making trips into Nashville—Hix allegedly spent weekends with his family—and there were few, if any, restrictions on visitors—once word got out that two convicted murderers were enjoying all the comforts of home, at taxpayers' expense, the *Chattanooga News–Free Press* ran an editorial on February 11, 1954, calling for an end to the "improper practice of letting murderers out of prison to a virtual 'vacation resort' at the pump house."

Nell Ammons Dixon, the sister of the murdered J. H. Ammons, wrote to Clement imploring him to "see that men like Hix and Helton are kept behind bars where they belong."[51] He replied in an earnest, stiffly worded letter, assuring her that there would be no recurrence of this situation: "I shall endeavor at all times to merit the faith and confidence you have placed in me and trust you will never have cause to be sorry for your trust in my administration."[52] Hix and Helton kept their positions as trusties but were reassigned to the prison hospital. Clement then ordered that, for the foreseeable future, all outside visits by prisoners be banned. For the state's anti-Clement faction, still bitter over his decisive gubernatorial victory and liberal political agenda, allegations of lax security at the state penitentiary offered the perfect opportunity to expose his and Edwards's inability to keep the general population safe.

Unfortunately for Clement and Edwards, the Hix/Helton controversy was but one of a number of recent security breaches that provided fodder for the opposition. The inmate Sam Reed Scruggs took some time off from his thirty-four-year sentence for holding up a string of liquor stores to visit his victims, asking them for character references for his upcoming parole hearing. The convicted murderer Freddie Crabtree, who had been working as a trusty at Eastern State Hospital, used his time away from the penitentiary to regularly visit his family, behavior that might have continued undetected had he not been arrested for stealing hogs.

More significant, the convicted murderer Roy Stallard, accompanied by a prison guard, had taken a state vehicle for a nearly five-hundred-mile round trip from Nashville to Kingsport, Tennessee, to meet with potential parole sponsors. Stallard, a former Hawkins County sheriff's deputy, was serving ninety-nine years for the robbery slaying of a used auto dealer, Alvin Rentfro, of Cleveland, Tennessee. His trip to Kingsport soliciting support for his parole was not his first—a week before Christmas he had made a similar trip to Morristown, Tennessee, and the previous August he had done the same in Cleveland. When first asked about the incident Edwards denied that Stallard had been given permission to go to Morristown or Cleveland, recanting only when he realized that an assistant might have approved the trip without his knowledge. Clement publicly reprimanded Edwards for allowing Stallard to travel to Kingsport, and the warden admitted to the egregious mistake. Although the Stallard story was originally reported in the *Kingsport Times-News,* once the *Tennessean* found out, it was splashed across the front page: "Paper Reveals 3rd Side Trip For 'Jailed' Killer," with an equally disquieting subheadline that read, "Convicted Murderer Allowed to Make Pleas for Parole." The article noted that State Institutions Commissioner Keith Hampton had issued a directive "[requiring] direct permission from [the] Commissioner for outside visits by state prison inmates," a restriction that excluded the Prisonaires: "Hampton said the quartet [*sic*], consisting of four long-term Negro convicts, will be allowed to continue booking engagements for personal appearances outside the prison."[53] An editorial in the same edition of the *Tennessean* ratcheted up the outrage, accusing Hampton of "[leaving] the impression that nothing much was wrong. . . . [He has not] offered any explanation of this outrageous coddling of cold-blooded killers sentenced to long terms. Nor has he indicated that he thinks any is due."[54]

The final straw occurred on the night of February 13, 1954, the day after the Stallard story appeared in the *Tennessean.* The prison guards Jack Massengill and Tom Turner, on an errand to return a film that had been screened for the inmates, agreed to take along the convicted murderer James "Iceman" Maxwell, who had lied to Massengill by telling him that Warden Edwards had approved of him tagging along. Why the guards agreed to take Maxwell in the first place remains a mystery, although it's not unreasonable to speculate that Maxwell was part of an elaborate sting to embarrass Clement. On the drive back to prison, Maxwell suggested they stop for some food at a barbeque stand run by his brother. A photographer and reporter from the *Tennessean* who just happened to be there ambushed them and, after collecting enough incriminating evidence, followed them back to the penitentiary. The next day the story was front-page news.

The controversy over security lapses put an immediate halt to the Prisonaires' touring and recording. Despite the exclusion granted to them by Commissioner Hampton, Clement simply could no longer risk his commitment to penal reform by allowing the group to continue performing publicly under such intense scrutiny and negative press. And while he remained convinced that the Massengill, Turner, and Maxwell debacle was an organized attempt to embarrass his administration, he was initially reluctant to leave a paper trail stating so. The same day the *Chattanooga News–Free Press*'s excoriating editorial appeared, Clement received a letter from the Reverend A. J. Campbell of the Tennessee Regular Baptist, Methodist, and Episcopal Convention requesting that the "Prison Airs" [*sic*] be permitted to perform in Memphis and Jackson, Tennessee, on behalf of the J. L. Campbell School of Religion. Clement took two weeks to respond, but an early draft, written by a staff member, contained a paragraph expressing Clement's and most likely Edwards's real feelings regarding the motive behind those critical of the administration: "I know how much warden Edwards would like to let you have the services of this fine quartet, however, due to recent efforts of politically biased, anti-administration newspapers to smear Warden Edwards's record at the State Penitentiary, we felt necessary to refrain from booking engagements for the Prisonaires for an indefinite period of time. Warden Edwards will probably write you fuller details relative to this."[55]

Clement returned the draft with these suggestions: "Don't you think the second paragraph is a little dangerous politically as it could be lifted from this letter and put in print? Why not say this is left entirely up to Warden Edwards? He knows not to release the Prisonaires for engagements at this time." The letter that went to Reverend Campbell contained no mention of a conspiracy by politically biased anti-administration newspapers, but it did suggest that if Warden Edwards were contacted directly, "[He would] explain our policy in this connection to you."[56]

Although Clement felt it politically imprudent to express this sentiment in writing, publicly he could not control his combativeness. Calling a press conference at the penitentiary the Monday after the barbeque ambush, Clement, flanked by Edwards and Hampton, adopted a tone that managed to be both contrite and accusatory. While admitting that Massengill and Turner flagrantly violated the warden's orders and had suffered the consequences—Massengill was fired on the spot, and Turner resigned a few days later—he characterized the *Tennessean*'s alleged scoop as a deliberate attack on his administration. "Every citizen owes it to his or her conscience," he urged, "to decide whether [it] was a mere coincidence or whether it was deliberately planned in order to obtain the dismissal of the warden and to discredit the Governor."[57] When asked if he would consider firing Edwards, Clement said he would if and only if "it were found that he violated orders or carried on the affairs of the prison in an immoral or illegal manner contrary to established prison practice."[58]

The press's accusations that the penitentiary's trusty system was riddled with abuse carefully elided any reference to the slipshod supervision commonplace during Gordon Browning's administration and

Swafford's tenure as warden, abuses that Edwards addressed almost from his first day on the job. Clement expressed this sentiment in a letter to a concerned constituent: "Although Warden James Edwards has not initiated any new practice in regard to granting prisoners excess liberty," he wrote, "he did make a mistake by the continuation of certain practices handed down to him. Mr. Edwards now realizes he used poor judgment in permitting a few prisoners to make a few trips outside the walls."[59] More informally, in a letter to his close friend Harry Miller, Clement reiterated this stand, saying, "The Warden has done nothing new, but very frankly, some of the practices carried over by this Administration which were inherited were not good ones and when brought to my attention, I have attempted to curtail them."[60]

Clement's damage control was swift and sure, effectively neutralizing the controversy and making it abundantly clear that he was in charge. His press conference concluded with a four-point reform plan for the state penitentiary: a captain of the guards would be appointed to supervise prison employees, a main entrance gate would be constructed to control traffic flow, the institution of a more comprehensive guard training program, and the appointment of a prison advisory committee for state penal institutions. The following day the pro-Clement *Banner* lauded the changes: "[The reforms] are well conceived and provide a substantial starting point to rectify an institutional weakness which would handicap the prison operation under the best stewardship obtainable."[61]

The imbroglio rallied Clement's close friends and political allies. "Good going, boy!" enthused Bill Forbes, "I'm delighted at the stand you're making in the prison case. Sure there is [*sic*] some reforms needed, but Rome wasn't built in a day. Radical changes takes [*sic*] careful and wise planning." Forbes, the executive secretary of the Nashville Home Builder's Association, affirmed his unwavering support for the governor: "Keep up the good work and I'll be personally happy to do whatever I can to help you back up on the hill for the next four years."[62] Two days after his dramatic press conference, Clement received an ornately worded, emotionally charged letter from the inmate Pal Shoaf. "[Warden Edwards], by his own intestinal fortitude, lifted the hopes of many of life's lesser fortunates from the gutters of despair to human beings of initiative and ambition heretofore never attempted in Tennessee penology," he enthused. "The Skipper's [Edwards] genial human-humane interest at all times, even to the least of us, has engendered a respect and loyalty few prison heads have ever achieved."[63] The Prisonaires "indefinite" hiatus from public appearances lasted only a few months. As ostensibly reformed criminals and model prisoners, they were the messengers of the potential of prison reform and, whenever possible, needed to be out in the community proselytizing this message.

Once the Hix/Helton controversy died down another recording session was scheduled, but this time, rather than court controversy, Clement and Edwards thought it best if Phillips traveled to Nashville. On May 8, Phillips, accompanied by Jud, took his cumbersome two-track portable recording equipment to the penitentiary and cut two songs: two takes of "What'll You Do Next?" written by Johnny, and "There Is Love in You," written by Johnny and Stewart. "What'll You Do Next?" is energetic and, at a mere 1:41, short and snappy but would have been immeasurably better had Phillips recorded it with a band as good as, say, Ike Turner's Kings of Rhythm. On the other hand, "There Is Love in You," the only song Johnny wrote with Stewart, is another beautifully rendered ballad (Stewart is credited as lead vocalist, but the falsetto sounds like Johnny) that ultimately sounds a step or two behind the R&B zeitgeist. But not having a single since the previous November forced Phillips's hand, and on July 1 "There Is Love in You" and "What'll You Do Next?" was released. It received positive, albeit perfunctory, reviews in the music trades and a few spins on WLAC and WSOK but overall garnered little interest and modest sales. It was the Prisonaires' fourth release on Sun. It would also be their last.

The same week the Prisonaires' final single was released Elvis Presley, Scotty Moore, and Bill Black met in Memphis for the first time. There was some awkward small talk, a little music was played, and an agreement reached that the three would reconvene the following evening at 7:00 p.m. at 706 Union Avenue with Phillips. That session, on July 5, 1954, started tentatively, with Elvis earnestly covering songs like Bing

Crosby's "Harbor Lights" and Leon Payne's "I Love You Because." After hours of takes and retakes yielding little more than some pleasant, if unobtrusive, pop songs, the three tired, frustrated musicians and their equally tired and frustrated producer, started cutting loose on Arthur "Big Boy" Crudup's "That's All Right [Mama]." As Moore told Guralnick, "All of a sudden, Elvis just started singing this song, jumping around and acting the fool, and then Bill picked up his bass, and he started acting the fool, too, and I started playing with them. Sam, I think, had the door to the control booth open—I don't know, he was either editing tape or doing something—and he stuck his head out and said 'What are you doing?' And we said, 'We don't know.' 'Well back up,' he said, 'try to find a place to start and do it again.' "[64]

On Wednesday, July 7, 1954, one day shy of a year since the release of "Just Walkin' in the Rain," Phillips met with his unrelated namesake, the Memphis disc jockey and tastemaker Dewey Phillips, the excitable, hyperverbal host of one of the most popular radio shows in the city on WHBQ. Sam played Dewey the tape of Elvis singing "That's All Right [Mama]." "[Dewey] was reticent and I was glad that he was," Phillips told Guralnick. "If he had said 'Hey man, this is a hit, it's a hit,' I would have thought [he] was trying to make me feel good. What I was thinking was, where you going to go with this, it's not black, it's not white, it's not pop, it's not country, and I think Dewey was the same way . . . he loved the damn record, but it was a question of where do we go from here?"[65] The next afternoon Phillips cut acetates, delivered them to WHBQ, and called Elvis to tell him that Dewey would most likely play them on his show that night—which he did. "The response," notes Guralnick, "was instantaneous. Forty-seven phone calls, it was said, came in right away, along with fourteen telegrams—or was it 114 phone calls and 47 telegrams?—he played the record seven times in a row, eleven times, seven times over the course of the rest of the program. In retrospect it really doesn't matter; it seemed as if all of Memphis was listening."[66] Although no one in the moment could have imagined or predicted the enormity of its generational scope, one thing was abundantly clear: music—pop, R&B, rockabilly, rock and roll—and youth culture would never be the same.

The emergence of Elvis did not by itself lead to the demise of the Prisonaires. The signs had been increasingly obvious with the apathetic public response to every release after "Just Walkin' in the Rain." To his credit, however, Phillips didn't simply give up on them after Elvis's spectacular debut. That same summer he brought the group to Sun and cut four songs: "Two Strangers," "Friends Call Me a Fool," "Lucille, I Want You," and the please-parole-us-paean "What about Frank Clement (A Mighty Man)." Finally conceding that the group needed more instrumental weight than simply Stewart's guitar, Phillips, on Johnny's recommendation, used backing musicians from the prison orchestra: the drummer Hubbard Brown, the pianist Henry "Dish Rag" Jones, the trumpeter George Williams, and an uncredited guitarist that some speculate was not an inmate but Joe Hill Louis. Phillips assigned matrix numbers to what was to be the next single, "Two Strangers," another weepy ballad by Riley, and "Friends Call Me a Fool," written by Johnny and Riley, a song which, as much as anything they wrote and recorded, comes closest to capturing the emotional depth of "Just Walkin' in the Rain," thanks mainly to Johnny's astonishing lead vocal. Understandably, Phillips would never have considered the Clement tribute a suitable single, but his reasons for not releasing "Lucille, I Want You," full of rough-and-tumble, gutbucket R&B charm, remain a mystery.

The final recording session by the Prisonaires, in late 1954, reveals a group struggling to reinvent itself. The three songs that came out of it are tougher, raucous, and, at times, more salacious than anything they had previously cut, but in the end they sound like indifferently recorded R&B simulacra. "Surleen," written by Johnny about his old girlfriend Jenny Price ("Surleen / she's good / but she's mean") chugs along in a manner not unlike Wynonie Harris's "Good Rockin' Tonight," but so do the other tracks, "All Alone and Lonely" and the sexually suggestive "Rockin' Horse," in which the lead vocalist Sanders sings about how much he "needs something to straddle."

In the end, Phillips, preoccupied by the changing face of R&B and rock and roll in a post-Elvis world, canceled the release of "Two Strangers" and "Friends Call Me a Fool." He needed little convincing that this experiment had run its course; there was nothing more to be gained aesthetically or commercially from the Prisonaires. Even so, years later he reflected somewhat regretfully on his mishandling of what he perceived to be a golden opportunity: "I think if I had more time to record the Prisonaires I really honestly believe we could have come up with a number of really big records. . . . the Prisonaires had a shot to be something . . . but I never achieved what they deserved in [terms of] potential."[67]

CHAPTER SEVEN

What'll You Do Next?

I'm very proud of [the Prisonaires], and I miss that. There's some things you can't forget [and now] they're all gone.

—Johnny Bragg

Marcel Sanders and John Drue were the first Prisonaires to be paroled. Sanders, who had refused release a year earlier, was effectively thrown out of the penitentiary on October 6, 1954. Drue, whose application for parole had been denied, was now deemed sufficiently rehabilitated and released. Proving the accuracy of his pessimistic preliminary inmate assessment, Drue violated the terms of his parole when he and an accomplice, Jack Birdsong, broke into the Kenneth O. Lester Company produce house and stole four hundred pounds of frozen chickens. Convicted of larceny and of receiving and concealing stolen property, Drue was sentenced to one to three years and returned to the penitentiary in early February 1955. He was paroled again in February 1957, this time with better results, as he never again spent a day behind bars. William Stewart, whose only crime was being in the wrong place at the wrong time when Benny White beat Robert Lauderdale to death, had his sentence commuted from ninety-nine years to life, which allowed for his immediate release. State Attorney General Baxter Key and Judge John A. Mitchell wrote to Governor Frank Clement on October 21, 1954, unequivocally recommending commutation to life and parole when eligible. Having served fifteen years, Stewart was released on April 15, 1955.

While Stewart's commutation and release received little media scrutiny, Clement's decision to commute Ed Thurman's ninety-nine-year sentence to life, thereby making him too eligible for immediate parole, was far more controversial. Convicted of first degree murder in the death of John Will Hardimon, Thurman, who had acted in self-defense, was released two weeks after Stewart. "We have never believed that a man that gets into a fight and kills another Negro in an argument should be sentenced to 99 years," noted the secretary of the parole board, Charles Crow. "The sentence is usually 2 to 10 years and sometimes 10 to 20 years. We thought the jury was a little tough in this case."[1]

From Clement's perspective, Thurman's commutation involved little political risk in that he had already won the Democratic primary renomination for governor (once again over his old foe Gordon Browning) by the widest margin in Tennessee history and had been reelected to the state's highest office by a similar margin of victory. "Never before in Tennessee politics," gushed the *Nashville Banner,* "has a young man demonstrated such tremendous strength as the 34-year-old Dickson Countian. . . . Tennessee believes in his capacity for dedicated stewardship [and] the effective and efficient administration of the state's business."[2] With the governor's term newly expanded from two to four years, Clement felt perfectly comfortable dipping into his sizeable cache of political equity to parole Thurman.

Needless to say, the *Tennessean* was outraged by the commutation of Thurman's sentence, its indignation prominently displayed in an overheated editorial published on April 29:

> Granted that a good tenor voice is an asset in some respects, it is startling now to find that it entitled a convicted murderer to his freedom after serving only 15 years of a 99-year prison sentence.
>
> That, however, seems to be the only plausible explanation for the release granted Edward L. Thurman, a member of the Prisonaires singing group which stands in so high with Governor Clement. . . .
>
> . . . [There] is nothing in his files to warrant his return to decent society after so brief a period. And in setting aside the sentence that Thurman received in the due course of justice, the governor and the parole board have flagrantly abused their authority. . . .
>
> Obviously the jury which heard the case did not think that the [sentence] was a "little tough" for a cold-blooded killer. Nor did the trial judge, who rejected a plea for a new trial. And neither did the Tennessee Supreme Court when the case was appealed to the high tribunal.
>
> Now, however, Governor Clement and the three-man parole board have taken it upon themselves to say that the jury, the trial judge and the Supreme

> Court were all wrong. They can cite no new evidence, and they can produce no recommendations for clemency from the officials of the county—Davidson—in which Thurman was convicted and sentenced. Instead they only say that he has "become a Christian" and they are convinced that he will be a "valuable citizen."
>
> Thus, assuming the responsibility of judge and jury, they decree that this man with a talent for murder as well as music shall go free. . . .
>
> . . . On this basis, the people of Tennessee can only hope that the killers still behind bars are non-singers.[3]

Stewart and Thurman were not the last Prisonaires to have their sentences commuted by Clement. The "sixth" member, Robert Riley, co-writer of "Just Walkin' in the Rain," had his ten-to-sixteen-year sentence for house breaking and larceny commuted and was paroled on October 22, 1956.

And then there was Johnny Bragg.

After the release of so many of the original members, Johnny continued to lead prison vocal groups but not under the name the Prisonaires. First calling themselves the Sunbeams but quickly changing the name to the Marigolds, the group had, according to Johnny, "[a] different sound—we did less gospel, more country, some pop . . . [the] Marigolds was mostly an update of the Prisonaires."[4] The group released a couple of singles on Ernie Young's Excello label, but only "Rollin' Stone," written by Riley and released in April 1955, made the charts, rising into the R&B Top 10. Johnny's life and career were more profoundly altered, however, on January 16, 1959, when Clement, as he had done for Stewart and Thurman, commuted his ninety-nine-year sentence to life and recommended immediate parole. Echoing the finding of the Pardons and Paroles Board, the governor concluded that the thirty-two-year-old inmate "has rehabilitated himself sufficiently to return to society."[5] An article in the *Banner* proclaimed Johnny to be "a natural born entertainer who puts his heart and soul into his work," also noting that, in their heyday, the Prisonaires "have been constant performers at the Governor's mansion. . . . [F]ew official functions occurred there at which they did not appear."[6]

The success of "Just Walkin' in the Rain" is mentioned in the *Banner* article, but the song's popularity is attributed only to Johnnie Ray, Johnny Bragg, and Riley. Riley is identified not by name but simply as "another inmate," but he and Johnny were said to have "gained [a] national reputation *for writing* [the song]" (emphasis added). The article further noted that Johnny was the last of the original group to still be in prison and that his songwriting and recordings "have brought a substantial amount of money which is now being held in trust for him."[7] While the statement is certainly true, Red Wortham, who held the copyright on "Just Walkin' in the Rain," admitted to taking more than his rightful share of the publishing and mechanical royalties. Released on January 28, 1959, Johnny used his notoriety as a singer to leverage a position as a staff songwriter with Tree Music and, with help from the producer Owen Bradley, secure a recording deal with Decca. Given all he had been through and the fact that he had a sizeable bank account (thanks mainly to Ray), he was in an enviable position for an ex-con about to restart his career in the music business.

A year later the *Banner* ran another story about Johnny, but it was not about his career as an entertainer. He had been arrested and jailed, charged with breach of the peace and driving with an expired registration. According to Johnny, he had been out "night clubbing" and, while stopped at a red light on the corner of Church Street and 13th Avenue, was sideswiped by a black car driven by a young white woman later identified as Patsy Huff Johnson (referred to in the *Banner* as "an attractive blonde-haired woman, [her age] estimated . . . to be about 20") who had hurriedly left her home after quarreling with her husband. Johnny chased her into east Nashville and located her car parked near the intersection of Gallatin Road and Trinity Lane. The two exchanged words, and Johnny left the scene after a patrol car with two Nashville police officers, who had been alerted to the chase, drove by. Johnson claimed she had pulled over to retrieve her purse, which had fallen to the floor of the car when Johnny confronted her. She told the officers she had been accosted by "a short, stocky negro," and within fifteen minutes Johnny had been apprehended. Not helping his version of events was the fact that the investigating officers could find no damage to his vehicle. As Sergeant T. M. Sesler told the reporter from the *Banner,* "He definitely hasn't been hit by a black car." Far more ominously, the article noted that, while in custody, "Johnny would be questioned . . . in several 'morals' cases. They declined to elaborate."[8] Police investigation into Johnny's involvement in these morals cases—allegations of sexual assault and robbery, some spurious, others credible—led to charges but no convictions. Johnny was certainly no saint and often seemed to be in the wrong place at the wrong time, but he was not a one-man crime wave.

The case involving Johnson proved to be far more complicated. Johnny was charged with breach of the peace and violation of the state automobile registration law. The accusation seemed flimsy, but, when coupled with the prosecutor's zealous insistence that the incident was part of a disturbing pattern of events and his constant references to Johnny's earlier rape conviction, it was enough to convince a jury that he was potentially dangerous and in violation of his parole.

In an interview with Colin Escott, Johnny averred that, like the rape conviction, this was a setup. "A man whose name I can't say," Johnny told Escott, "said, 'If that bible-totin' governor turns that nigger loose, I'll get him back inside even if I have to frame him.' [They] finally got me on a charge of stealing $2.50—and I had all kinds of money. It was pitiful."[9] Convicted and sentenced to five years for robbery, Johnny returned to the state penitentiary in the spring of 1960.

A year later came a second encounter with Elvis, although unlike the "accidental meeting" at Sun during the session that produced "Just Walkin' in the Rain," this one was verified and documented by parties other than Johnny himself. The *Banner* reported that "en route home to Memphis after Wednesday's visit to the State Legislature, singer-actor Elvis Presley stopped for approximately 45 minutes at the State Prison. He toured the various workshops, [the] dining hall, and death-house, and talked briefly with songwriter Johnny Bragg, who is doing time for a parole violation."[10] "Ain't that something?" Johnny recalled decades later. "I went out there and grabbed him, he hugged me. 'Johnny,' he said, 'what can I do for you? You want me to see the Governor right now? I'm going to get you out of here. I want you out of here.'" According to Johnny, Elvis offered to cover any legal expenses and, in a gesture that might have afforded Johnny a lifetime of financial security, suggested he record "Just Walkin' in the Rain." "You want me to record it," Elvis told him, "just let me know [and] I'll do it."[11]

Denied parole on May 5, 1965, Johnny was not granted his release until November 3, 1967. He went to work at Woodlawn Cemetery in Nashville, eventually quitting his job to go into business with his supervisor, Raymond Liggon, and Liggon's friend Sewell Jackson, forming the independent record label Elbejay. But by December 1969 Johnny was in trouble again, this time caught sitting in a car with a friend who was in a compromising position with a young, white prostitute. Arrested on one count of aiding and abetting prostitution, a parole violation, he was sent back to prison in January 1970. This trip would be short-lived, as the Board of Pardons and Paroles granted him his third release on February 4, 1970. Don McGehee, the director of the Division of Probation for the State Department of Corrections, was outraged at what he perceived to be preferential treatment for a chronic recidivist. "It's disgusting," he angrily told a reporter for the *Banner*. "He's still in the prison and he is going to be there until we have a favorable psychiatric evaluation on him."[12] Johnny's impending parole proved equally unpopular with other inmates, who "voiced resentment to the board's actions arguing that they have been turned down for parole and Bragg has been handed his freedom three times." In the end, disgust, resentment, and psychiatric evaluations would not prevent Johnny from leaving prison for a third time, on May 12.

During this period Johnny met his wife, Gail Green, a white woman twenty years his junior, from east Tennessee. They married soon after Johnny's parole, and in 1971 she gave birth to a daughter whom they named Misti. Johnny was still writing and recording for Elbejay but would return to prison in April 1977 when Gail was attacked by a man Johnny thought was a street thug but who was in reality an off-duty Nashville police officer and former boyfriend of Gail's who took exception to her marriage to a black ex-con. Unaware of this at the time, Johnny disarmed the man and left with Gail, only to be arrested later and charged with shoplifting. Although Johnny was clearly not the instigator but was burdened by a criminal record that included multiple parole violations, the white officer's fallacious accusation, despite being contradicted by a number of eyewitnesses, held sway, and Johnny was sentenced to sixty days in the county workhouse. After being remanded to the state penitentiary to await his hearing because the shoplifting charge was considered to be another parole violation, Gail, who had been in poor health, died. In August Johnny was moved from the prison back to the county workhouse to complete the remainder of his sixty-day sentence. Released on August 22, 1977, he would never again return to prison.

After his final parole Johnny never reestablished himself as a performer or songwriter and, as he grew older, seemed content working, as he put it, "as a full-time family man" to his daughter and grandson, his only regular singing gig being Sunday church services. In 2000 he briefly appeared in the A&E Network television documentary *Sam Phillips: The Man Who Invented Rock and Roll,* singing a portion of "Just Walkin' in the Rain" in front of his old cell in the now-abandoned state penitentiary. His voice sounds weathered but strong, his phrasing and enunciation fluid and crisp, his falsetto still poignant. This spontaneous public performance would be his last—four years later Johnny Bragg died of cancer at the age of seventy-nine.

As for the other Prisonaires, their trails vanished into the ether. Riley worked as a contract songwriter writing soul, R&B, and country songs in Nashville, but the rest of the group, in Escott's words, "died in varying states of poverty or distress," never again working in the music industry. Stewart drifted into chronic drug addiction and alcoholism, dying of a heroin overdose in 1959. All that is known of Sanders is that he ended up back in prison in 1965 on a burglary conviction, was paroled in 1967, and died shortly thereafter. Thurman was killed in a car accident on April 5, 1973, and Drue succumbed to cancer on December 11, 1977.

After his reelection, Clement began building a national reputation as the political face of a new, progressive, modern South, a South that slowly and reluctantly was coming to grips with the undoing of Jim Crow segregation mandated by the U.S. Supreme Court's ruling in 1954 in *Brown v. Board of Education.* In 1956 he was handpicked to deliver the keynote address before a nationally televised audience at the Democratic National Convention in Chicago and gave a "rousing, old-fashioned, Tennessee stump speech attacking the Republicans." Clement accused President Dwight D. Eisenhower and Vice President Richard Nixon of running a reelection campaign steeped in slander and half truths. And while there were those who found his rhetorical flourishes inspiring, others were "repulsed by [his] attacks, his stump speech style and his emphatic mannerisms. The speech was a failure. In a mere 43 minutes, Clement had ended his national political hopes."[13] The Tennessee state constitution prohibited Clement from running for a consecutive four-year term, and he was succeeded by his former campaign manager, Buford Ellington, who essentially kept the governor's mansion warm until Clement could run again in 1962, which he did, easily defeating the Republican candidate Hubert Patty in the general election. Ellington would again succeed Clement as governor in 1967, leading critics to refer to this unprecedented gubernatorial back and forth as the "leapfrog government." After two unsuccessful bids for the United States Senate in 1964 and 1966, Clement was considering another run for governor in 1969. But his dream of returning to the state's highest office ended abruptly on the night of November 4, when the car he was driving collided with another vehicle on Franklin Road in Nashville. Pronounced dead at the scene, Frank Clement was only forty-nine years old.

Clement's old friend James "Droopy" Edwards was one of the pallbearers at his funeral two days later in Dickson. As crucial a figure as Clement in allowing the Prisonaires to be heard outside of the state penitentiary, Edwards had decided early in his tenure as warden that the constant pressure and intense scrutiny that accompanied running the state's largest prison were simply too much to bear. In 1956, after a little more than three years on the job, he resigned for a considerably less stressful and more lucrative position in industrial relations at the Ford Glass Plant in Nashville. He retired in 1981 and moved to Murfreesboro, Tennessee, residing there until his death at the age of eighty-three in 2001.

In his book *Lipstick Traces,* Greil Marcus observed that what remained irreducible about punk rock was its desire to change the world, a desire that "begins with the demand to live not as an object but as a subject of history—to live as if something actually depended on one's actions—and that demand opens onto a free street."[14] This observation could just as easily describe the events that occurred to the Prisonaires, beginning with the summer of "Just Walkin' in the Rain" and ending during the summer of Elvis and "That's All Right [Mama]." One could reasonably quibble with the notion that the Prisonaires' music was embedded with a "desire to change the world"; such an idea implies a willfulness that Johnny Bragg and Robert Riley likely did not have in mind as they wondered what the little girls were doing while walking to their prison laundry jobs on that rainy day. But neither can "Just Walkin' in the Rain" be glibly dismissed (despite the best efforts of Johnnie Ray, Mitch Miller, and Ray Conniff) as simply an innocuous pop song, the kind of commodified emotionalism that the conservative semanticist and pop music hater S. I. Hayakawa famously proclaimed "tends toward wishful thinking, dreamy and ineffectual nostalgia, unrealistic fantasy, self-pity, and sentimental clichés masquerading as emotion."[15] It is, rather, a song that, in the hands of men who have little else, becomes a source of purpose and power, a demand to live not as an object but as a subject of history—living as if the creation of this enclave of autonomy depended entirely on their actions. It may not have been enough to tear down the prison walls, but it was enough to alter their lives as inmates and provide them with limited opportunities of public expression denied to most men in similar situations.

Not so mysteriously, then, the story of the Prisonaires and "Just Walkin' in the Rain," despite its "one-hit-wonder" status, never completely vanishes from the lexicon of popular music culture; it remains a fascinating story revealing the complex and transformative powers of pop music. It is rare in the ecology of poplore for a species to be extinguished; rather, it leaves glimpses, traces, a musical palimpsest wherein the overwritten words are once again legible, indicating the dialogic adaptability, as opposed to the total disappearance, of vernacular culture. After Ray's spectacularly successful version of 1956, the song was covered in 1962 by the country singer Jim Reeves, who remained faithful to the laborious, cluttered Conniff arrangement, and again in the mid-1970s by the Welsh-born neorockabilly singer Michael Barratt, more popularly known as Shakin' Stevens, who eschewed subtlety and nuance for big, meaty guitars. More recently, Eric Clapton, oddly enough, chose to cover it for a

Sun Records tribute recording in 2001, and the bohemian avant-gardist Tom Waits, in his capacity as guest editor of the two hundredth issue of the British music magazine *Mojo,* selected the Prisonaires' recording for inclusion on an accompanying CD. "The Prisonaires," wrote Waits, "possess a sense of vocal melancholia which they'd clearly [earned]." [16]

But of all the recent reappearances of the Prisonaires in popular culture, perhaps the most spectacular was in Jonathan Lethem's novel of 2003 *Fortress of Solitude.* The protagonist, Dylan Ebdus, a smart, slightly nerdy white kid insouciantly raised by his boho/hippie parents in a predominantly black section of Brooklyn, is so overwrought and fixated on his terrible childhood that he has enormous problems getting on with the business of living an adult life. Dylan carves out something resembling a career as an underpaid and underappreciated music journalist and author of liner notes. In the concluding third section of the novel, set in the fall of 1999 and entitled "The Prisonaires," Dylan is in the office of the executive Jared Orthman of DreamWorks Pictures pitching him the Prisonaires' story. "A thousand or a million writers hungered for what I have today," Dylan thinks to himself. "I hoped not to blow it, not so much on [the Prisonaires'] behalf as on that of my own shriveled prospects and swollen debt."

Lethem's description of the pitch hilariously and accurately reveals both the market-driven nature of Hollywood and the tone-deafness of its executives. Nervous and close to hyperventilating, Dylan is trying to reveal the salient facts of the Prisonaires' story to a constantly interrupting Orthman.

> "Let me set it up." I'd been advised to "talk in scenes." "I'd want to start the movie inside the prison. The lead Prisonaire is a guy named Johnny Bragg. He's the songwriter, the lead singer. He's been in jail for years, since he was sixteen. On trumped-up charges. So he and another convict are out in the yard, walking, in the rain, literally, and one says to the other. 'Here we are, walking in the rain, I wonder what the little girls are doing?' And Johnny Bragg starts singing the line, a mournful little song, 'Just Walkin' in the Rain.' Which became their first hit. Maybe it could be played over the opening credits."
>
> "That reminds me of something else."
>
> "You're probably thinking of 'Singing in the Rain.' "
>
> "Oh yeah, sure. He wrote that?"
>
> "Different song."
>
> "Okay, let me get this: he's wrongfully imprisoned. What's the charge?"

"Well, actually it was six convictions for rape. Six ninety-nine-year sentences with no possibility of parole."

"Ouch."

"The cops set him up. He was an arrogant, good-looking kid, and they had it in for him. They pinned a bunch of unsolved rapes on him."

"Brad Pitt. Matthew McConaughey."

"I forgot to say black."

"These are *black people?*"

"Yes."

"Okay." Jared waved his hands, reluctantly brushing Pitt from the room. "Start again with the black people. How does he get out of jail?"[17]

After agreeing to Dylan's request for five "uninterrupted" minutes, Orthman becomes increasingly animated, punctuating Dylan's descriptions with the names of suitable, black leading men ("I don't know if you'll like this, but I'm totally picturing Denzel Washington"). He's not terribly fond of the real life ending—too unresolved and unspectacular, a whimper instead of a bang—so he suggests the film's climactic set piece be the staging of a massively successful Prisonaires' comeback, to which Dylan, though fully aware of the preposterous, contrived nature of the suggestion, agrees. "What further harm would a little comeback bring?" he thinks, "Or a big one?" The pitch now reaches a sexualized crescendo until, at the point of ecstatic release, Dylan tells Orthman that Johnny Bragg is still alive. Almost immediately, a film project that seconds earlier seemed destined for a green light screeches to a halt. Orthman's mood becomes gloomy, fatalistic: "He appeared to be recovering from some sort of bender, coming down as after an orgasm or a hit of crack." A live Johnny Bragg presents problems, the studio would have to option his life rights, a process that, Orthman notes, "can get really sticky"; that reality, along with an uncertain ending, seals the project's fate. The film would never live up to the one that Orthman envisioned in his head during Dylan's pitch; it wasn't "a slam-dunk," it wasn't "airtight."[18]

If Hollywood were to film the Prisonaires' story, it would be reminiscent of other filmic attempts at writing pop music history: fact-fudging, emotionally simplistic, histrionic, uncomplicated renderings of complex, paradoxical lives and times, with an uplifting ending unimpeded by reality. The pantheon of celluloid romans à clef includes *The Buddy Holly Story*, *La Bamba*, *American Hot Wax*, and *Cadillac Records*—these are the Jared Orthman–approved history of pop music. The Prisonaires' story, however, resonates *because* of its imperfections and nuance. Like any good narrative or song, the hook is compelling: imprisoned men using music as a means of cultural and personal survival. But it is also a story imbued with the irony that incarceration leveraged their musical career, allowing them limited, supervised access to the outside world, all of this set into motion by the creation of one remarkable song. Helped along by a governor and a warden who, perhaps naively and self-servingly, saw the group as a means to a political end and a record producer who gradually understood how powerful a gesture "Just Walkin' in the Rain" really was. This is the music of what Cornel West refers to as "prisoners of hope," those who use hope as a method of combating despair. To be hopeful in this instance doesn't necessarily generate optimism, but "the energy to be courageous, to bear witness, to see what the end is going to be."[19]

That movie would be remarkable.

NOTES

Prologue: Poor Old Johnnie Ray

1. Jonny Whiteside, *Cry: The Johnnie Ray Story* (New York: Barricade Books, 1994), 78.
2. Richard Severo, "Mitch Miller, Maestro of the Singalong, Dies at 99," *New York Times,* August 2, 2010.
3. Ibid.
4. Whiteside, *Cry: The Johnnie Ray Story,* 222. In his capacity as Ray's biographer, Whiteside is equally glib and dismissive of "Just Walkin' in the Rain": "[Johnnie Ray and Mitch Miller] were, in a sense, both right. It really [was] a piece of crap: trite, simplistic, sub-Ink Spots stuff. Johnnie gave it an appropriately on-the-money, straight pop delivery, and Mitch had the last laugh."
5. Joseph Lanza, *Elevator Music* (New York: St. Martin's Press, 1994), 103.
6. Peter Guralnick, *Last Train to Memphis: The Rise of Elvis Presley* (New York: Little Brown, 1994), 57–58.
7. Colin Escott, liner booklet essay for the Prisonaires, *Just Walkin' in the Rain,* issued as Bear Family BCD 15523, compact disc.
8. W. E. B. Du Bois, *The Souls of Black Folk* (New York: Bantam [1903]; Definitive Jubilee Edition reprint, 1989), 182.

1. Nashville

1. *Nashville Daily American,* April 25, 1880.
2. Don Doyle, *Nashville in the New South 1880–1930* (Knoxville: University of Tennessee Press, 1984), 63.
3. Ibid., 235. Bobby Lovett, "Black Bottom," Tennesseeencyclopedia.net/entry.php?rec=1565.
4. Bobby Lovett, *The African American History of Nashville, Tennessee, 1780–1930* (Fayetteville: University of Arkansas Press, 1999), 84.
5. Doyle, *Nashville in the New South,* 41.
6. Ibid., 99.
7. Don Doyle, *Nashville since the 1920s* (Knoxville: University of Tennessee Press, 1985), 42.
8. Lovett, *The African American History of Nashville, Tennessee,* 74.
9. Charles Wolfe, *A Good Natured Riot: The Birth of the Grand Ole Opry* (Nashville: Vanderbilt University Press, 1999), 28. Doyle, *Nashville in the New South,* 80.

10. Lovett, *The African American History of Nashville,* 74.
11. Wolfe, *A Good Natured Riot,* 28.
12. Bruce Nemerov, liner essay, *John Work, III: Recording Black Culture,* Spring Fed compact disc, 2007.
13. Bill Malone, *Singing Cowboys and Musical Mountaineers: Southern Culture and the Roots of Country Music* (Athens: University of Georgia Press, 1993), 16.
14. Marshall Wyatt, "Violin Sing the Blues For Me: African American Fiddlers on Early Phonograph Recordings," www.oldhatrecords.com
15. John Hartley Fox, *King of the Queen City: The Story of King Records* (Champaign: University of Illinois Press, 2010), 5.
16. Bill Malone, *Country Music U.S.A.,* 2d rev. ed. (Austin: University of Texas Press, 2002), 104.
17. Malone, *Singing Cowboys and Musical Mountaineers,* 88–89.
18. "Biggest Colored Dance of the Year," advertisement, *Nashville Tennessean,* August 10, 1937.
19. Doyle, *Nashville in the New South,* 115, 130.
20. Doyle, *Nashville since the 1920s,* 49–50.
21. John Gordon Gay, "Negro Dependency and Delinquency in the Southern Community" (MA thesis, Vanderbilt University, 1926), 19.
22. Ibid., 37.
23. Ibid., 46.
24. Doyle, *Nashville since the 1920s,* 45.
25. Randall Shelden, "From Slave to Caste Society: Penal Changes in Tennessee, 1830–1915," *Tennessee Historical Quarterly* 38, no. 4 (1979): 465
26. Ibid.
27. Robert Spinney, *World War II in Nashville: Transformation of the Homefront* (Knoxville: University of Tennessee Press, 1998), 54.

2. The Prisonaires

1. William Stewart, Tennessee Department of Corrections inmate file.
2. Robert Riley, Tennessee Department of Corrections inmate file.
3. John Edward Drue, Tennessee Department of Corrections inmate file.
4. Ibid.
5. Marcel Sanders, Tennessee Department of Corrections inmate file.
6. Ibid.
7. Sterling Brown, "Negro Folk Expression," in *A Son's Return: Selected Essays of Sterling Brown,* ed. Richard Yarborough (Boston: Northeastern University Press, 1996), 239.
8. Lawrence Levine, *Black Culture and Black Consciousness: Afro American Folk Thought from Slavery to Freedom* (New York: Oxford University Press, 1977).
9. Johnny Bragg, interview by Don Hildebrand and Barry Alphonso, Nashville, TN, transcribed September 25, 1996, Cassell Productions, Thousand Oaks, California.
10. Ibid.
11. Ibid.

12. Ted Gioia, *The History of Jazz* (New York: Oxford University Press, 1997), 179.

13. Johnny Bragg, interview by Hildebrand and Alphonso.

3. The Prison, the Governor, and the Warden

1. Nicolas Fischer Hahn, "Female State Prisoners in Tennessee: 1831–1979," *Tennessee Historical Quarterly* 39, no. 4 (1980): 485; Bernie Sheahan, "Hot Homes," *Nashville Scene,* November 18, 1993; Clark Parsons, "Pulling the Switch," *Nashville Scene,* November 18, 1993.

2. Michel Foucault, *Discipline and Punish: The Birth of the Prison* (New York: Vintage, 1979), 238; "History of the Auburn Correctional Facility: The Best Prison in the World," www.geocities.com/MotorCity/Downs/3548/facility/auburn.html

3. Foucault, *Discipline and Punish,* 238.

4. Flogging of prisoners under the Auburn system was originally authorized by the state of New York in 1819.

5. "History of the Auburn Correctional Facility: The Best Prison in the World," www.geocities.com/MotorCity/Downs/3548/facility/auburn.html

6. Leon Faucher, quoted by Michel Foucault, *Discipline and Punish,* 242.

7. "The Prison Discipline Society," www.simmons.edu/libraries/archives/char_coll/char_coll001.htm

8. Randall G. Shelden, "From Slave to Caste Society: Penal Changes in Tennessee, 1830–1915," *Tennessee Historical Quarterly* 38, no. 4 (1979): 464.

9. H. Bruce Franklin, *The Victim as Criminal and Artist* (New York: Oxford University Press, 1979), 101.

10. Shelden, "From Slave to Caste Society," 465

11. Ibid., 463, 467.

12. Larry E. Sullivan, *The Prison Reform Movement: Forlorn Hope* (Boston: Twayne Publishers, 1990), 38.

13. Blake McKelvey, *American Prisons: A Study in American Social History Prior to 1915* (1936; reprint Glen Ridge: Patterson Smith, 1972).

14. "Warden Uses Prisonaires as Example of Humane Policy," *Ebony,* November 1953, 48.

15. John Szwed, *Alan Lomax: The Man Who Recorded the World* (New York: Viking, 2010), 39.

16. Ibid., 37–38.

17. Alan Lomax, *The Land Where the Blues Began* (New York: Pantheon, 1993), 262.

18. Szwed, *The Man Who Recorded the World,* 51.

19. Ibid., 45.

20. Ibid., 59.

21. Mary L. Cohen, "Choral Singing and Prison Inmates: Influences of Performing in a Prison Choir," *Journal of Correctional Education* 60, no.1 (2009): 52–65.

22. "New VH-1 Series Explores Jailhouse Rock," *Los Angeles Times,* October 18, 2002.

23. "Jailhouse Rock," *Entertainment Weekly,* October 1, 2002.

24. Peter Guralnick, *Last Train to Memphis: The Rise of Elvis Presley,* 419.

25. www.musicfromthebighouse.com

26. "New VH-1 Series Explores Jailhouse Rock," *Los Angeles Times,* October 18, 2002.

27. Lee Seifert Greene, *Lead Me On: Frank Goad Clement and Tennessee Politics* (Knoxville: University of Tennessee Press, 1982), 3, 17; William L. Davis, "Frank Clement: The First Campaign," *Tennessee Historical Quarterly,* 35, no.1 (1976): 84.

28. Greene, *Lead Me On,* 39–40.

29. Ibid, 3, 194. Despite a ruling by the Tennessee Supreme Court that reduced the power of the clause banning interracial marriages, the wording remained in the state constitution until 1978.

30. It is indeed odd, if not downright illogical, that of Nashville's two daily newspapers the conservative *Banner* was far more sympathetic to Clement that the more liberal *Tennessean.* This was owing primarily to the failure of the Republican Party in Tennessee to produce a candidate the paper could support. Even though Clement was too liberal by the *Banner*'s standards, he was conservative enough (in a field of far less appealing conservative Democrats) for the paper to endorse. The *Tennessean*'s animus toward Clement was the result of his affiliation with the powerful Memphis Democrat Edward Hull "Boss" Crump, a sworn enemy of the publisher of the *Tennessean,* Silliman Evans.

31. Greene, *Lead Me On,* 71–72.

32. "Attorney to Succeed Swafford," *Nashville Banner,* January 10, 1953. "Edwards to Use MP Experience," *Nashville Tennessean,* January 11, 1953.

33. John M. Sloop, *The Cultural Prison: Discourse, Prisoners, and Punishment* (Tuscaloosa: University of Alabama Press, 1996), 32.

34. "Warden Edwards Tightens Control on His Charges," *Nashville Banner,* March 18, 1953. James Edwards, telephone interview by author, Richmond, VA, May 18, 1996.

35. Ibid.

36. Johnny Bragg interview, Rodger Jacobs, untitled Prisonaires / Johnny Bragg documentary script draft, copyright 2005–2006, Cassel Productions.

37. Bragg interview, Hildebrand and Alphonso.

4. Men Singing Together

1. Johnny Bragg interview, Rodger Jacobs, untitled Prisonaires / Johnny Bragg documentary script draft, copyright 2005–2006, Cassel Productions.

2. Ibid.

3. Ian Chambers, "A Strategy for Living: Black Musicians and White Subcultures," in *Resistance through Ritual,* ed. Stuart Hall and Tony Jefferson (London: Unwin Hyman, 1976), 161.

4. George Lipsitz, *Time Passages: Collective Memory and American Popular Culture* (Minneapolis: University of Minnesota Press, 1990), 115.

5. Bragg interview, Jacobs.

6. Ibid.

7. Lee Seifert Greene, *Lead Me On: Frank Goad Clement and Tennessee Politics* (Knoxville: University of Tennessee Press, 1982), 191.

8. James Edwards, telephone interview by author, Richmond, VA, May 18, 1996.

9. Johnny Bragg, interview by Don Hildebrand and Barry Alphonso, Nashville, TN, transcribed September 25, 1996, Cassell Productions, Thousand Oaks, California.

10. "Exchange Club Has Brilliant Service Record," *Nashville Banner,* August 5, 1936.

11. "Warden Cites Prison Improvements," *Nashville Banner,* June 17, 1953.

12. Ibid.

13. Prisonaires "live" recording, Tennessee State Penitentiary, ca. late 1950s, recording courtesy of Jonathan Clark, February 2009.

14. Ibid.

5. Music City, USA

1. Craig Havighurst, *Air Castle of the South: WSM and the Making of Music City* (Champaign: University of Illinois Press, 2007), 2.

2. "WLAC Radio," NashvilleBroadcastingHistory.com.

3. William Barlow, *Voice Over: The Making of Black Radio* (Philadelphia: Temple University Press, 1998), 161.

4. John Ortizano, "Negro Appeal Radio Stations Using a Rhythm and Blues Format," AEJMC conference paper, December 3, 1996, list.msu.edu/cgi-bin/wa?2=ind9612a&l=aejmc&d=1&P=32866. According to Ortizano, John Richbourg's show drew an average of fifteen million listeners, making it one of the most popular radio shows not just in Tennessee but in the Southeast.

5. Havighurst, *Air Castle of the South,* 14.

6. Michael Kosser, *How Nashville Became Music City, U.S.A.: Fifty Years of Music Row* (Milwaukee: Hal Leonard Publishing, 2006), 3.

7. Bruce Feiler, *Dreaming Out Loud: Garth Brooks, Wynonna Judd, and the Changing Face of Nashville* (New York: Harper Perennial, 1999), 89.

8. Don Doyle, *Nashville since the 1920s* (Knoxville: University of Tennessee Press, 1985), 153–54.

9. Robert Gordon and Bruce Nemerov, eds. *Lost Delta Found: Rediscovering the Fisk University–Library of Congress Coahoma County Study, 1941–1942* (Nashville: Vanderbilt University Press, 2005), 24–26. Acknowledging that Work's legacy has suffered from indifference and that his "research and analysis have been appropriated by others," Gordon and Nemerov go on to note, "When [Alan] Lomax published [*Land Where the Blues Began*] in 1993, John Work is mentioned three times; in the preface, he was mentioned in association with the musical transcriptions; in the sole text mention, he was present at the recording of Muddy Waters; in the acknowledgements his name is listed with [Lewis] Jones and [Samuel] Adams."

10. Martin Hawkins, *A Shot in the Dark: Making Records in Nashville, 1945–1955* (Nashville: Vanderbilt University Press 2006), 9–12.

11. Ibid., 19–29.

12. Ibid., 49.
13. Ibid., 70.

6. "Just Walkin' in the Rain"

1. Colin Escott, liner booklet essay for the Prisonaires, *Just Walkin' in the Rain,* issued as Bear Family BCD 15523, compact disc.
2. Johnny Bragg, interview by Don Hildebrand and Barry Alphonso, Nashville, TN, transcribed September 25, 1996, Cassell Productions, Thousand Oaks, California.
3. Ibid. Escott exhibits little skepticism regarding Bragg's audacious claim of having written "Your Cheatin' Heart." "It is at least possible," Escott writes, "that Williams bought the genesis of the song from Bragg as he bought other songs that he made uniquely his own." This theory, however, is not repeated in his biography of Hank Williams of 1993.
4. Bill Malone, *Singing Cowboys and Musical Mountaineers: Southern Culture and the Roots of Country Music* (Athens: University of Georgia Press, 1993), 90.
5. Ibid., 92.
6. Holly George-Warren, *Public Cowboy No. 1: The Life and Times of Gene Autry* (New York: Oxford University Press, 2007), 277.
7. Ibid., 280–81.
8. Brian Ward, *Just My Soul Responding: Rhythm and Blues, Black Consciousness, and Race Relations* (Berkeley: University of California Press, 1994), 82.
9. Robert Pruter, *Doo Wop, the Chicago Scene* (Champaign: University of Illinois Press, 1996), xii.
10. Ibid.
11. Bob Hyde, liner essay, *The Doo Wop Box,* Rhino compact disc 71463, 1993.
12. Nelson George, *The Death of Rhythm and Blues* (New York: Plume, 1988), 36.
13. Ward, *Just My Soul Responding,* 56.
14. Ibid., 57.
15. John Hartley Fox, *King of the Queen City: The Story of King Records* (Champaign: University of Illinois Press, 2010), xv.
16. Ibid., 1.
17. George, *Death of Rhythm and Blues,* 40.
18. Ward, *Just My Soul Responding,* 50.
19. Hyde, *The Doo Wop Box.*
20. Ray Pratt, *Rhythm and Resistance: The Political Uses of Popular Music* (Washington: Smithsonian Institution Press, 1990), 22.
21. Ward, *Just My Soul Responding,* 81.
22. The idea that reality is mediated by language and that language is mediated by reality is liberally appropriated from Stuart Hall.
23. Mikhail Bakhtin, *The Dialogic Imagination: Four Essays* (Austin: University of Texas Press, 1981), 324–25.
24. W. T. Lhamon Jr., e-mail correspondence with the author, May 6, 1996. Lhamon explores this idea in greater detail in *Deliberate Speed: The Origins of a*

Cultural Style in the American 1950s (Washington: Smithsonian University Press, 1990), 48–50.

25. Erving Goffman, *Asylums: Essays on the Social Situations of Mental Patients and Other Inmates* (New York: Doubleday / Anchor, 1961), 38.

26. Thomas McLaughlin, *Street Smarts and Critical Theory: Listening to the Vernacular* (Madison: University of Wisconsin Press, 1996), 38.

27. Ibid.

28. W. E. B. Du Bois, *The Souls of Black Folk* (New York: Bantam [1903]; Definitive Jubilee Edition reprint, 1989), 186.

29. Martin Hawkins, *A Shot in the Dark: Making Records in Nashville, 1945–1955* (Nashville: Vanderbilt University Press 2006), 107.

30. Ibid., 204.

31. Sam Phillips interview, Rodger Jacobs, untitled Prisonaires / Johnny Bragg documentary script draft, copyright 2005–2006, Cassel Productions.

32. Ibid.

33. Ibid.

34. "Sam Phillips: Sun Records—The Man Who Invented Rock and Roll," www.elvis.com.au/presley/articles_samphillips.shtml

35. Bragg interview, Hildebrand and Alphonso.

36. Colin Escott and Martin Hawkins, *Good Rockin' Tonight: Sun Records and the Birth of Rock and Roll* (New York: St. Martin's Press, 1991), 60–61.

37. Sam Phillips interview, Rodger Jacobs.

38. Anna Belle Clement interview, Rodger Jacobs, untitled Prisonaires / Johnny Bragg documentary script draft, copyright 2005–2006, Cassel Productions.

39. Ibid.

40. Sam Phillips interview, Rodger Jacobs.

41. "Stock Car Races Tonight Help Kids To Play," *Nashville Tennessean,* July 9, 1953.

42. "Prisoners May Find Fame With Record They Made in Memphis," *Memphis Press-Scimitar,* July 18, 1953.

43. "The Prisonaires: Unique Singing Group of Tennessee Prisoners Finds Fame on Radio, Television, and Records," *Ebony,* November 1953.

44. Maurice Haste, letter to James Edwards, August 15, 1953.

45. "The Prisonaires," *Ebony,* November 1953.

46. "Prisoner Hangs Himself in Cell," *Nashville Tennessean,* July 26, 1953.

47. Escott, *Just Walkin' in the Rain,* liner booklet essay.

48. "Prisonaire Before Parole Board Wednesday," *Nashville Banner,* September 9, 1953.

49. "Prison Singers Left Unguarded," *Nashville Tennessean,* December 26, 1953.

50. "Bad Judgment by Prison Officials," *Chattanooga News–Free Press,* February 11, 1954.

51. Nell Ammons Dixon, letter to Frank Clement, February 13, 1954.

52. Frank Clement, letter to Nell Ammons Dixon, February 16, 1954.

53. "Paper Reveals 3rd Side Trip for Jailed Killer," *Nashville Tennessean,* February 12, 1954.

54. Editorial, *Nashville Tennessean,* February 12, 1954.

55. Frank Clement, letter to Rev. A. J. Campbell (first draft), February 23, 1954.

56. Frank Clement, letter to Rev. A. J. Campbell (final draft), March 1, 1954.

57. "Clement Orders 4-Point Reform Program for State Penitentiary," *Nashville Banner,* February 15, 1954.

58. Ibid.

59. Frank Clement, letter to J. M. Dunlap, February 23, 1954.

60. Frank Clement, letter to Harry Miller, March 2, 1954.

61. Editorial, *Nashville Banner,* February 16, 1954.

62. William Francis Forbes, letter to Frank Clement, February 26, 1954.

63. Pal Shoaf, letter to Frank Clement, February 16, 1954.

64. Peter Guralnick, *Last Train to Memphis: The Rise of Elvis Presley* (New York: Back Bay Books, 1994), 95.

65. Ibid., 99.

66. Ibid., 100.

67. Sam Phillips, interview Rodger Jacobs.

7. What'll You Do Next?

1. "Songbird Out of Cage," editorial, *Nashville Tennessean,* April 29, 1955.

2. "Clement Wins Great Victory in Tennessee," *Grapevine,* September 1954.

3. "Songbird Out of Cage," April 29, 1955.

4. Johnny Bragg, interview by Don Hildebrand and Barry Alphonso, Nashville, TN, transcribed September 25, 1996, Cassell Productions, Thousand Oaks, California.

5. "Clement Commutes Prisonaire's Term," *Nashville Banner,* January 16, 1959.

6. Ibid.

7. Ibid.

8. "Walkin' in the Rain Composer Jailed," *Nashville Banner,* January 18, 1960.

9. Colin Escott, liner booklet essay for the Prisonaires, *Just Walkin' in the Rain,* issued as Bear Family BCD 15523, compact disc.

10. Ibid.

11. Johnny Bragg interview, Rodger Jacobs, untitled Prisonaires / Johnny Bragg documentary script draft, copyright 2005–2006, Cassel Productions.

12. "Parole OK for Bragg Criticized," *Nashville Banner,* February 4, 1970.

13. "Frank G. Clement," Alan Griggs, *Tennessee Encyclopedia of History and Culture,* tennesseeencyclopedia.net/imagegallery.php?EntryID=C107

14. Greil Marcus, *Lipstick Traces: A Secret History of the Twentieth Century* (Cambridge: Harvard University Press, 1989), 3–4.

15. S. I. Hayakawa, "Popular Songs vs. the Facts of Life," *Etc.: General Review of Semantics* 12 (1955): 83–95.

16. Tom Waits, *Mojo,* no. 200, July 2010.

17. Jonathan Lethem, *Fortress of Solitude* (New York: Vintage, 2003), 323–30.

18. Ibid., 334–36.

19. Cornel West, interview, *Rolling Stone,* November 15, 2007.

INDEX

Song Titles

"All Alone and Lonely," 99
"Baby Please," 3, 76, 84
"Band of Gold," 3
"Bear Cat," 2
"Blue Moon," 68
"Coming Home," 85
"Crazy Blues," 13
"Don't Say Tomorrow," 91
"Dreaming of You," 76
"Friends Call Me a Fool," 99
"Harbor Lights," 98
"I Know," 89–90
"I Love You Because," 98
"I Wish," 91
"If I Didn't Care," 4, 68
"If I Had You," 2
"If I Were King," 88
"In The Candlelight," 2
"It's Too Soon to Know," 4, 68
"Johnnie's Coming Home," 1
"Just Walkin' in the Rain," 2–7, 51, 65, 67, 76–77, 88, 91, 99, 103, 107, 109; creation of, 71; internal/external analysis, 72–75; Elvis Presley's offer to record, 105; as proto-doo-wop, 68–69; recording of, 78–81; release of, 82; sales of, 84, 87
"Lead Me On," 83
"Light Up," 40
"Little Old Log Cabin in the Lane," 13
"Look Homeward Angel," 2
"Love Me Tender," 5
"Lucille, I Want You," 99
"The Missouri Waltz," 83
"My God is Real," 87–88
"Nashville Jumps," 62
"Near You," 63, 84
"No More Tears," 87–89, 91
"The Old Hen Cackled and the Rooster's Going to Crow," 13
"The Old Rugged Cross," 83
"Please, Please, Please," 70
"A Prisoner's Prayer," 71, 87–90
"Rocket 88," 3, 87
"Rockin' Horse," 99
"Rollin' Stone," 103
"Softly and Tenderly," 87–88
"Surleen," 99
"That's All Right (Mama)," 98, 109
"That Chick's Too Young to Fry," 76
"That Lucky Old Sun," 1
"Two Strangers," 99
"Weaker Than Wise," 2
"What about Frank Clement (A Mighty Man)," 99
"Your Cheatin' Heart," 65
"Zeb's Mountain Boogie," 62

General Index

Abramson, Herb, 69
Acuff, Roy, 59, 64
Acuff-Rose Publishing Company, 59
Allen, Austin and Lee, 14
Allen, Bill "Hoss," 57, 84
Allen, Governor O. K., 39
American Federation of Musicians strike, 61

American Hot Wax (film), 111
American Society of Composers, Authors, and Publishers (ASCAP), 59
Ammons, J. H., 92
Andrew Jackson Courts, 27
Armstrong Louis, 15, 57
ASCAP. *See* American Society of Composers, Authors, and Publishers
Askew, John C., Jr., 30
Atlantic Records, 69–70
Auburn system, 6, 31–35, 45, 54
Autry, Gene, 65–67
Avalon, Frankie, 71

Bailey, DeFord, 12
Baird, James, 90–91
Barrasso, Anselmo, 14
Barratt, Michael (Shakin' Stevens), 109
Basie, Count, 28
Bennett, Tony, 2–3
Berle, Milton, 75
Berry, Chuck, 40
Big Three Trio, 63
Bijou Theater for Negroes, 14
Billboard (magazine), 1, 5, 63, 85, 87–88
Birdsong, Jack, 101
Bissey, Christopher, 40
Black, Bill, 97–98
Black Bottom (Nashville neighborhood), 10–12
Black Legion, 27
black radio, 70
Black Samson, 38
Bobby's Record and Tape Center, 69
Bond, Johnny, 67
Boston Prison Discipline Society, 33
Bradley, Owen, 62, 104
Bragg, Billy, 41
Bragg, Johnny, 3, 4, 6, 19, 48–51, 64, 89, 109; arrests in 1969 and 1977; attempt on life in prison, 52; childhood and events leading to imprisonment, 25–30; as co-composer of "Just Walkin' in the Rain," 71; commutation of sentence, 103; death of, 107; final release from prison, 107; impact of incarceration on songwriting, 74; and Patsy Huff Johnson, 104–5; meeting with Elvis Presley in 1961, 105; as Prisonaires spokesman and musical director, 67; second release from prison, 106; third release from prison, 107
Bragg, Maybelle, 26
Bragg, Misti, 106
Bragg, Wade, 26–27
Brassell, Bob, 50
Brenston, Jackie and His Delta Cats, 3, 87
Broadcast Music Incorporated (BMI), 59
Brockman, Polk, 13
Brown, Hubbard, 99
Brown, James, 40, 70
Brown, Sterling, 25
Brown v. Board of Education, 50, 107
Browning, Gordon, 43–44, 95, 102
Brushy Mountain Penitentiary, 22
The Buddy Holly Story (film), 111
Bulleit, Jim, 60–63, 75, 84
Bullet Recording and Transcription Company, 61, 75; "sepia series," 62
Buttram, Pat, 66

Cadillac Records (film), 111
Calloway, Cab, 28
Calloway, Joe, 76
Campbell, Reverend A. J., 94
Caravan Music, 66
Carlisle, Cliff, 13–14
Carson, "Fiddlin'" John, 13
Cash, Johnny, 40
Cashbox (magazine), 85, 87–88
Cedar Street (Nashville), 10–11, 15
Cedarwood Publishing, 59
Charioteers, 67
Chattanooga Free-Press, 92, 94
Cherry, Don, 2
Chess Records, 70
Chicago Defender, 68
Chiarelli, Rita, 41
Clapton, Eric, 109
Clement, Anna Belle, 83

Clement, Frank, 4, 6, 38–39, 46–47, 49, 54–55, 76, 83–84, 90–91, 97; correspondence with A. J. Campbell, 95; correspondence with constituents, 96; death of, 108; Democratic Convention keynote address, 107; and Democratic party, 42–43; education, 42; first gubernatorial campaign, 43–45; opposition to death penalty, 51; reelection, 102; reprimand of Edwards, 93; response to Hix/Helton controversy, 92–94
Clooney, Rosemary, 2
Cobb, David, 58
Cohen, Paul, 77
Cohn, David, L., 37
Colored Ladies Relief Society, 15
Colored Masonic Home, 15
Conniff, Ray, 2–5, 74–75, 109
Cooke, Sam, 71
Copas, Cowboy, 64
Crabtree, Freddie, 93
Craig, Edwin W., 58
Craig, Frances, 63
Crawford Street (Nashville), 10–11, 15
Crosby, Bing, 97–98
Crosby, David, 40
Crow, Charles, 86, 102
Crudup, Arthur "Big Boy," 98
Cumberland University, 42
Curtis, King, 70

Darby, Tom, 13
Davis, Jimmie, 13–14
Day, Doris, 2
Decca Records, 77, 104
Delany, Mary Joy, 92
Denno, Wilfred L., 86-87
Dixie Hummingbirds, 91
Dixon, Nell Ammons, 92
Dixon, Willie, 63
doo-wop, 68–69, 71
Dorms, Lee "Blabbermouth," 77
Drake, 40
Drue, John Edward "Junior," 3, 5, 51; death of, 107; events leading to imprisonment, 22–23; parole hearing, 89–90; parole and return to prison, 101
Duane, Jimmy, 4–5
Du Bois, W. E. B, 7, 15, 75
Dwight, Louis, 33

Earle, Steve, 40
Ebdus, Dylan, 110–11
Ebony (magazine), 4, 84–87
Edwards, Curley (and the Georgia Peach Pickers), 61
Edwards, Evelyn, 76, 83
Edwards, James, 4, 6, 39, 54–55, 76, 84–86, 89–91, 97; appointment as warden, 45; arranging rehearsals for Prisonaires, 49–50; death of, 108; penal philosophy, 45–47; resignation as warden, 108; speech to Nashville Exchange Club, 52–53
Eisenhower, Dwight D., 107
Elbejay Records, 106
Ellington, Buford, 108
Ellis, Hattie, 38, 41
Emerson, Henry, 16–18
Ernie's Record Mart, 62
Escott, Colin, 4, 64, 81, 105, 107, 118n3
Everett, Vince, 40–41
Excello (record label), 103

Fabian, 71
Fairfield Four, 62
Faucher, Leon, 32
Feathers, Charlie, 70
Fisk University, 12, 15, 27, 56
"5" Royales, 85
Folsom Prison, 40
Forbes, Bill, 96
Fortress of Solitude (Lethem). 110
Franklin, Bruce H., 34
Frazier, Nathan "Ned," 12, 59

Gant, Cecil, 62
Gay, John Gordon, 16–17, 26
Gellert, Lawrence, 36
George, Nelson, 68

Gilbert, Charles, 30
Gliva, Al, 41
Goffman, Erving, 74
Golden West Melodies, 66–67
Goodman, Benny, 28
Gore, Bertha, 22
Grandmaster Flash and the Furious Five, 70
Grand Ole Opry, 12, 58–59, 64, 75
Green, Douglas, 65
Green, Gail, 106–7
Griffin, Bessie, 49
Guralnick, Peter, 3, 40, 81, 98

Hadacol Caravan, 75
Haines, Augustus, 27
Haines, Mattie, 27
Haley, Alex, 70
Hall, Raymond, 14
Hammond, John, 28
Hampton, Keith, 93–94
Hardimon, John Will, 19, 102
Harris, Wynonie, 63, 68, 99
Haste, Maurice, 85
Havighurst, Craig, 56
Hawkins, Martin, 60, 63
Hay, George D., 58
Hayakawa, S. I., 109
Hell's Half Acre (Nashville neighborhood), 10
Helton, Eugene, 92
Henderson, Fletcher, 15
heteroglossia, 73
Hill and Range Songs, 59
Hippodrome (Nashville), 14
Hitchcock, Conrad Vertre (C. V.), 61, 63
Hix, Milton, 91
Hix/Helton controversy, 93–94, 97
Holiday, Billie, 27–28, 57, 81
Holloway, Ezell, 24
Hopalong Cassidy, 66
Hope, Bob, 75
Houck Piano Company, 60
Howell, "Peg Leg," 13
Howlin' Wolf, 77
Hurston, Zora Neale, 26

Ink Spots, 4, 51, 67–68, 82, 91
It's a Natural (record label), 69

Jackie Brenston and His Delta Cats, 3, 87
Jackson, Benjamin Clarence "Bull Moose," 68
Jackson, Sewell, 106
Jackson County Sentinel, 86
Jail Guitar Doors program, 41
Jailhouse Rock (film), 40
James, Elmore, 70
James, Harry, 2
J-B Records, 76
Jefferson, Blind Lemon, 13
Jet (magazine), 87
J. L. Campbell School of Religion, 94
John Daniel Quartet, 62
Johnson, Guy, B., 36
Johnson, Joe, 66–67
Johnson, Lonnie, 13
Johnson, Patsy Huff, 104–5
Johnson, Pete, 57
Johnson, Pickins "Picky," 49–50
Jones, Henry "Dish Rag," 99
Jones, James Robert, 22
Jordan, Louis, 57, 68
Jordanaires, 79
Josie Records, 69
Jubalaires, 88
Jubilee Records, 69

Keisker, Marion, 81
Kenny, Bill, 4, 51, 67–68
Kercheval, Thomas, 8–9
Key, Baxter, 101
King, B. B., 82, 85
King, Pee Wee, 62
King Records, 70
Kingsport Times-News, 93
Knight, Gladys (and the Pips), 70
Kramer, Wayne, 40–41

La Bamba (film), 111
Laine, Frankie, 2–3
Lake, Leola, 24

The Land Where the Blues Began (Work), 60, 117n9
Lauderdale, Robert, 21, 85, 101
Law, Don, 66
Lead Belly (Huddie Ledbetter), 38–39, 83
Leiber, Jerry, 40
Lethem, Jonathan, 110
Levine, Lawrence, 72
Lhamon, W. T., Jr., 73
Lieberson, Goddard, 2
Liggon, Raymond, 106
Lil Wayne, 40
Lipsitz, George, 49
Lomax, Alan, 37–39, 60
Lomax, John, 37–39
The Lone Ranger, 66
Longhorn Records, 41
Louis, Joe Hill (Leslie Hill), 82, 97
Louis Buckley's Record Shop, 62
Louisiana Hayride, 75
Lovett, Bobby, 11

Malone, Bill, 12
Marcels, 68
Marcus, Greil, 108
Marigolds, 103
Marquette Prison Band, 41
Mascot Company, 65
Massengill, Jack, 94–95
Mathis, Johnny, 2–3
Maxwell, James "Iceman," 94
McAlister, Harry Hill, 38
McDonald, Bruce, 41
MC5, 40
McGehee, Don, 106
McLaughlin, Thomas, 75
McPhatter, Clyde, 71
Memphis, 3, 70, 79, 87
Memphis Commercial Appeal, 4, 81
Memphis Press-Scimitar, 4, 84
Memphis Recording Service, 78
Miller, Harry, 96
Miller, Mitch, 1–2,4–5, 67, 74–75, 109
Mills Brothers, 77, 82
Mitchell, John A., 101
Modern Records, 70
Mojo (magazine), 110
Monroe, Bill (and his Blue Grass Boys), 61
Moore, Scotty, 97–98
Morgan, George, 64
Murray, Albert, 12

Nashville, 3, 6, 79, 87, 92, 97, 106; African American population, 9–10; African American middle class, 15; African American youth, 15; centennial of 1880, 8–9; metamorphosis into Music City, USA, 57–60; and music history, 59; nightclubs, 60; and radio, 56
Nashville Banner, 4, 17–18, 30, 43, 84, 89, 102–6, 116n30
Nashville Colored Orphanages, 15
Nashville Exchange Club, 52–53, 77, 79, 82, 92
Nashville Tennessean, 4, 17–18, 30, 79, 84, 86, 91, 93–94, 102, 116n30
Nathan, Syd, 70
National Association of Broadcasters, 59
National Life and Accident Insurance Company, 58
Neff, Pat, 38
Nickelson, Celene, 29
Nix, Margaret Ruth, 24
Nixon, Richard, 107
Nobles, Gene, 57

Odum, Howard, W., 36
Okeh Records, 4, 12
Old Hickory Singers, 61
Old Town Records, 69
O'Reilly, Bill, 40
Orioles, 4, 68, 85
Orthman, Jared, 110–12

Paley, Cass, 19
Paramount Records, 13
Pardons and Paroles Board (Tennessee), 103, 106

Parker, Colonel Tom, 64
Parthenia (Johnny Bragg's grandmother), 26–27
Patterson, Frank, 12, 59
Patty, Hubert, 108
Payne, Leon, 98
Pearl, Minnie (Sara Ophelia Colley Canon), 56, 62
Peer, Ralph, 13
penal labor, 33–35
Phillips, Dewey, 98
Phillips, Jud, 87, 97
Phillips, Sam, 2, 5–6, 63, 70, 76–78, 83, 88–89, 91, 99–100; meeting with Dewey Phillips, 98; as producer, 80–81; recollection of Elvis at Prisonaires recording session, 81–82; travels to Nashville to record Prisonaires, 97
Pilgrim Travelers, 68
Plumber, Annie Mae, 19–20
Porteus, Clark, 81
Powell, "Bouncin'" Billy, 77
Powell, M. M., 22
Pratt, Ray, 71–72
Presley, Elvis, 2, 40, 64, 97–98, 105; alleged appearance at Prisonaires recording session, 81
Price, Jenny, 29, 99
Pride, Charley, 12
Prisonaires, 3–7, 23, 35–36, 42, 46, 48–49, 63, 88, 100, 109–12; career linked to lives as convicts, 71; Christmas Eve incident, 90–91; conduct as both accommodation and resistance, 53–54; criticism of performances, 86–87; events leading to imprisonment, 19–30; final recording session, 99; first recording session at Sun, 78–81; formation of group, 49–51; origin of name, 79; record deal with Sun, 77; as representative of prison reform, 54–55; performances at Governor's mansion, 83–84; performances outside prison, 85–86; singing at the death house, 50–51; as vernacular theorists, 74–75. *See also entries for individual members*
Proctor, James, 71, 88

Ra, Sun, 69
race music, 13
Randy's Record Shop, 62
Ravens, 68
Ray, Johnnie, 1–5, 67, 73, 75, 103, 109, 113n4
record business, state of in 1940s, 61
Red Robin Records, 69, 76
Reeves, Jim, 109
Republic Pictures, 65
Rentfro, Alvin, 93
Rhapsody in Black (film), 28
Richbourg, "John R," 57, 117n4
Rikers Island, 40
Riley, Robert, 4, 54, 67, 71, 82, 91, 107, 109; commutation of sentence, 103; events leading to imprisonment, 21
Robinson, Bobby, 69
Rodgers, Jimmie, 13, 65
Rose, Fred, 59
Ruby (Nashville police detective), 30
Rushing, Jimmy, 28

Sanders, Marcel, 3, 5, 51, 80, 99; death of, 107; events leading to imprisonment, 23–25; parole hearing, 89; parole, 101
San Quentin Prison, 40
Satherley, Art, 61
Savoy Records, 70
Scarborough, Dorothy, 37
Scott-Heron, Gil, 40
Scruggs, Sam Reed, 93
Sentimentalists, 67
Sesler, Sergeant T. M., 104
Shaffer, Ed, 14
Shoaf, Pal, 96
Sing Sing Prison, 86
Smith, Carl, 64
Smith, Mamie, 13
The Souls of Black Folk (Du Bois), 7
Spinney, Robert, 17

Spirits of Memphis Quartet, 70
St. Louis Jimmy, 63
Stallard, Roy, 93
Stanley Brothers, 70
Starr, Milton, 14
State of Tennessee v. John Henry Bragg, 30
Stewart, William, 3, 49–51, 82, 85–86, 99; commutation of sentence and release, 101–3; death of, 107; events leading to imprisonment, 20
Stoller, Mike, 40
Sunbeams, 103
Sun Ra, 69
Sun Records, 5, 76
Sun Studios, 3
Swafford, Glenn, 35–38, 44–45, 49–50, 64, 84, 95
Swan Silvertones, 68
Szwed, John, 37

Talley, Thomas, 59
Tardy, Fred, 86
Tarlton, Jimmie, 13
Tennessee Board of Pardons and Paroles, 103, 106
Tennessee State Board of Prison Commissioners, 17
Tennessee State Department of Corrections, 29, 72
Tennessee State Penitentiary, 3, 21, 26, 31, 35, 38, 54, 65, 67; percentage of African Americans in prison population, 17, 34–35; segregation within prison, 50
Tennessee State Training and Agricultural School, 22, 27
Tennessee Tech University, 85
Theater Owners' Booking Association (TOBA), 14
Thomas Rufus, 3, 77
Thompson, James Donald (Uncle Jimmy), 58–59
Thurman, Ed, 3, 5, 21, 49–51, 80; commutation of sentence controversy, 101–3; death of, 107; events leading to imprisonment, 19–20
Til, Sonny (Earlington Carl Tilghman), 4, 68, 89
Tree Music, 59, 104
Truman, Harry, 83
Tubb, Ernest, 62, 64–65
Turner, Ike (and the Kings of Rhythm), 77, 87, 97
Turner, Tom, 94–95
Turpin, Charles, 14

Vanderbilt University, 16, 42, 56, 66

WABV, 56
Wagon Wheel (Nashville), 14
WAIM, 60
Waits, Tom, 110
Waller, Fats, 57
Ward, Billy (and the Dominoes), 70
Ward, Brian, 67, 69
Washington, Denzel, 111
Watson, John Henry, 86
Watt, John, 85
WBAW, 56
WCBQ, 56
WDAA, 56
WDAD, 56
WDIA, 70, 82
WEBX, 56
Weiss, Hy, 69
West, Cornel, 112
Western Music (publishing company), 66
WHBQ, 98
Whirlin' Disc (record label), 69
White, Bennie, 21, 101
White, Crawford, 21
White, George, 77
White, Harding, 21
White, Newman I., 37
Whiteman, H. B., 29
Williams, George, 99
Williams, Hank, 65, 75, 81
Williams, Sherman, 63
Willis, Chuck, 85
Wills, William Ridley, 83
Wilson, Teddy, 28

Witt, R. Beecher, 44
WLAC, 56–57, 84, 97
Wolf, Howlin', 77
Wood, Randy, 62
Woodlawn Cemetery (Nashville), 106
Woods, Oscar, 14
Work, John Wesley, III, 12, 59
Wortham, Wilburn Clyde "Red," 76–77, 79, 104
WSIX, 56, 76–77, 79, 83
WSM, 56–58, 61
WSM Barn Dance, 12, 58
WSOK, 77, 84, 97

Young, Cal, 77
Young, Ernie, 62, 103
Young, Lester, 28

JOHN DOUGAN grew up in Brookfield, Massachusetts, and earned a PhD in American studies from the College of William & Mary. A former music journalist, he has published essays and reviews in numerous magazines, newspapers, and journals including *Rolling Stone, Spin, American Music,* and the *Journal of Popular Music Studies*. He is the author of the book *The Who Sell Out* (Continuum, 2006) and is currently professor of music business and popular music studies in the Department of Recording Industry at Middle Tennessee State University.